Architectural Drawings of the Russian Avant-Garde

Essay by Catherine Cooke

The Museum of Modern Art, New York

Distributed by Harry N. Abrams, Inc., New York

Architectural Drawings of the Russian Avant-Garde

Published on the occasion of the exhibition
"Architectural Drawings of the Russian Avant-
Garde," June 21–September 4, 1990, organized
by Stuart Wrede, Director, Department of
Architecture and Design, The Museum of
Modern Art

This exhibition is supported by a grant from
Knoll International, Inc. Additional funding
has been provided by Lily Auchincloss, The
International Council of The Museum of
Modern Art, the National Endowment for the
Arts, and the Trust for Mutual Understanding.

Photograph Credits: Plates from the
A. V. Shchusev State Research Museum of
Architecture, Moscow; text figures courtesy
C. Cooke, except nos. 10 and 26, The Museum of
Modern Art

Library of Congress Catalogue Card
Number 90-61320
Clothbound ISBN 0–87070–556–3
Paperbound ISBN 0–87070–556–3
Abrams clothbound edition ISBN 0–8109–6000–1

Edited by Janet R. Wilson
Designed by Janet Odgis & Company Inc.
Production by Pamela Smith
Type set by Sarabande Press, New York
Printed by Eastern Press, Inc., New Haven,
Connecticut
Bound by Sendor Bindery, New York

The clothbound edition distributed in the
United States and Canada by Harry N. Abrams,
Inc., New York, A Times Mirror Company.
Distributed outside the United States and
Canada by Thames and Hudson Ltd., London

The Museum of Modern Art
11 West 53 Street
New York, New York 10019

Cover: Ivan Leonidov, *Palace of Culture of the
Proletarsky District of Moscow. Center for
Physical Education,* 1930

Contents

The work of the Russian avant-garde during the years 1917 to 1934 constitutes an extraordinary chapter in twentieth-century art and architecture. From the outbreak of the Bolshevik revolution to the avant-garde's ideological demise under Stalin, it was a period when radical changes in the arts converged with social and political revolution.

Like most of its compatriot vanguard movements in Europe, the Russian avant-garde drew inspiration from the innovations of Cubism before World War I. And like these movements it fostered an intimate collaboration and cross-fertilization among the arts. Not only the fine arts and architecture but also photography, films, industrial design, and graphics thrived in this period. The Russians had their own unique talents in the artists Kazimir Malevich and Vladimir Tatlin, both of whom had a direct influence on architecture.

The accession to power of a revolutionary government that set about transforming the social order gave the architectural profession an opportunity, through competitions and commissions, to redefine architecture's social and cultural role. At the time these developments captured the imagination of modern architects internationally who, especially in Europe, were still functioning within an essentially conservative bourgeois social order. Among those who did work in Russia were Le Corbusier, Hannes Meyer, and Ernst May.

While this confluence of artistic and political revolution retains a strong hold on our imagination, it is not enough to account for the continuing powerful attraction of this architectural work. Rather, it is the formal inventiveness and high aesthetic level of the projects, as well as their range, that capture our attention today. Germany was perhaps the only other country in the 1920s with an equal number of architects committed to modernism. But unlike their generally "sachlich" approach, much of the Russian work displays a conceptual and structural daring that in the finest examples, such as the designs of Leonidov, ascends to a spiritual realm. Their work, however, belied the lack of a modern technical and material base to sustain these visions into built structures. Perhaps, as in the case of the Futurists in Italy, the country's technological backwardness was liberating.

Central to this spirit of daring innovation were schools such as the VKhUTEMAS with their open and experimental teaching program staffed by leading members of the various avant-garde groups. Equally if not more radical than the Bauhaus, the VKhUTEMAS was from the outset considerably more involved in the training of architects than was its German counterpart.

In her essay for this catalogue Catherine Cooke has admirably presented the richness of the theoretical and ideological debates both within the avant-garde as well as between its members and the emerging Socialist Realists. The arguments between a "rationalism" based on formal, spatial, and psychological considerations and one based on structural and functional concerns, as well as between modernists and traditionalists, seem to have a certain current relevance and cast the present-day architectural debates into perspective.

Inexplicably the first standard histories of modern architecture by Siegfried Giedion, Nikolaus Pevsner, and Henry-Russell Hitchcock left out the Russian avant-garde. Even Reyner Banham's seminal *Theory and Design in the First Machine Age* of 1960 barely touched on the subject. The difficulty of doing research in Russia at the time and the climate of the early cold war may have been partly to blame. The work was not rediscovered in the West until the 1960s with the publication of books such as Anatole Kopp's *Ville et revolution* (1967), as well as the 1970 landmark exhibition, "Art in Revolution," organized by the Arts Council of Great Britain at the Hayward Gallery in London. Since then an increasing number of articles and books in the West, and also by Russian scholars, notably S. O. Khan-Magomedov's *Pioneers of Soviet Architecture*, have helped provide a fuller and more detailed picture of this work.

Despite this increased attention, the projects of the Russian avant-garde architects have become familiar to us mainly through grainy black-and-white photographs. Not until recently have any of the original drawings been available for exhibition. The A. V. Shchusev State Research Museum of Architecture in Moscow, from whose archives we have been so generously allowed to select drawings for this exhibition, is the largest repository of such material in Russia, indeed in the world. While the Shchusev collection is not comprehensive, it is a most representative collection of the avant-garde architectural activity of this period and includes some of its finest work. Segments of the collection have been shown in Europe, but this is the first time the original drawings are on view in the United States, as well as the first time that all the most important drawings of the avant-garde period in the collection have been seen together in one exhibition. The work of some thirty-five architects is represented in the exhibition, another important testament to the scope of this remarkably creative period.

I am most grateful to the Shchusev State Research Museum of Architecture in Moscow for so generously lending us this unique collection of architectural drawings and to Igor Kazus, Acting Director, and Alexei Shchusev, former Director of the museum, for their enthusiasm and support in making the exhibition possible. I am equally grateful to Yevgeny Rozanov, Minister of the State Commission on Architecture and Town Planning, for his support.

It has been a particular pleasure to work with the curatorial and administrative staff of the Shchusev Museum. My thanks to Lev Lyubimov for his efforts in coordinating the work at the museum, to Marina Velikanova and Dotina A. Tuerina for helping to review the drawings in the archives and for preparing the initial checklist and architects' biographies, to Karina Yer Akopiar and Irina Chepuknova for showing me the drawings on my two initial visits and for so kindly introducing me to the avant-garde architecture in Moscow.

Special gratitude must go to Kevin Roche, who first told us about the drawing collection at the Shchusev and then generously provided the support for a first exploratory trip to Moscow to review the material.

At The Museum of Modern Art I am grateful to Richard Oldenburg, Director, for his efforts toward the realization of this exhibition. James Snyder, Deputy Director for Planning and Program Support, and Richard Palmer, Coordinator of Exhibitions, contributed vital administrative support for the project. I also wish to thank Sue Dorn, Deputy Director for Development and Public Affairs, and her staff; Jeanne Collins, Director of Public Information; Waldo Rasmussen, Director of the International Program, and Carol Coffin, Executive Director of the International Council; Ellen Harris, Deputy Director of Finance and Auxiliary Services; Aileen Chuk, Administrative Manager in the Registrar's office; Jerome Neuner and the exhibition production and framing staff; Michael Hentges, Director of Graphics; Joan Howard, Director of Special Events; and

Emily Kies Folpe, Museum Educator/ Public Programs. Their efforts have all been invaluable to the success of the exhibition and related events.

For their essential assistance in the preparation of the catalogue I am grateful to the staff of the Publications Department: Janet Wilson, Associate Editor, and Pamela Smith, Associate Production Manager, as well as Harriet S. Bee, Managing Editor; Tim McDonough, Production Manager; and Nancy Kranz, Manager of Promotion and Special Services. It has been an equal pleasure to work with Janet Odgis, the designer of this very handsome volume.

Special thanks to Catherine Cooke for the main catalogue essay, which elegantly places the architectural projects in the context of their time. In addition, she has served as a most valuable adviser to the exhibition. Igor Kazus has also contributed an informative history of the Shchusev Museum and its collection. Andrew Stivelman has provided translations from the Russian texts, biographies, and checklists. Magdalena Dabrowski, Associate Curator in the Department of Drawings, has been a valuable consultant on the Russian texts.

In my own department I am grateful to Marie-Anne Evans and Ona Nowina-Sapinski for their unfailing support, and to Matilda McQuaid, Christopher Mount, and Robert Coates for their help in the production of the exhibition.

Finally, of course, an exhibition and catalogue of this scope are not possible without the commitment of an enlightened sponsor. I wish to thank Knoll International, Inc., and its chairman, Marshall Cogan, for the enthusiastic support of this exhibition.

I am most grateful for additional support from Lily Auchincloss, and also from The International Council of The Museum of Modern Art, the National Endowment for the Arts, and the Trust for Mutual Understanding. The Contemporary Arts Council of The Museum of Modern Art has kindly provided support for the related symposium.

Stuart Wrede
Director
Department of Architecture and Design

Images in Context

by Catherine Cooke

In the social upheavals of the Russian Revolution in 1917, the architectural profession lost many of its most prominent clients, as aristocratic families fled from Petrograd and millionaire merchant dynasties disappeared overnight from Moscow. A certain percentage of the professional middle classes also left, but the majority struggled to make an existence, and where appropriate to make themselves useful, in the upside-down world that followed. As was again to be the case twenty years later under the purges of Stalin, most architects were adaptable enough to be able to continue to design and, when possible, to build. Buildings, like medical care, are always needed; changed social conditions and reduced technical options offered a fresh challenge within which imaginative and entirely professional responses remained valid. Behind the screen created by the seductive work of the avant-garde generation, therefore, lies an enormous and important continuity in architectural practice between the pre-revolutionary years and the twenties.

Russia had been very little urbanized before the Revolution. Its only settlements worthy to be called "cities" were the current and former capitals, St. Petersburg (renamed Petrograd in 1914) and Moscow, each having about two million inhabitants. Their nearest rivals, in cultural, artistic, and professional sophistication, were Kiev and Odessa, with populations of just over half a million. In terms of structural technique, buildings as advanced as any in Europe could be found, but these pockets of advanced building were extremely small. The image of the modern city and the industrial environment that generated it, which were such real inspiration for American and European modernism, were in general no part of the Russian population's experience

(fig. 1). The expansion of industrial development, the attempts to bring the essentials of modernity to the predominantly rural population, in the forms of literacy, numeracy, primitive agricultural machinery, and electric power, were to be the major campaigns of the later twenties.

On the eve of the First World War, however, Russia's economy was growing faster than that of any other in the developed world. Embryonic middle-echelon, professional, and proletarian groups were forming within the population but numerically hardly constituted "classes." What that growth might have meant had history been different is, of course, a matter of speculation. What happened in reality was that the growing embryo was aborted. It was to be a whole decade—through the First World War, the Revolution, and the subsequent Russian Civil War, then the mass famine and privations of 1921–24—before economists could speak of the building industry "waking up again after ten years asleep."[1] Most of the damage to the building stock of towns and cities was done during the Civil War, partly resulting from hostilities and partly from the gradual dismantling of buildings by an urban population seeking firewood for winter survival. Industry stood still and the population froze and starved as the Bolsheviks who had taken Petrograd and Moscow extended their victory over the Imperial forces, the so-called Whites, to the rest of the Russian continent.

Even more serious, for the long-term recovery period which the avant-garde generation would face, was the damage those ten years brought to the building-materials industry. Many of the technical preoccupations and obsessions with "economy of materials" that recur so frequently in avant-garde theory were generated as much by terrible shortages as they were by the influence of modernist aesthetics and design morality in Western journals, when these filtered into Russia again after the Western Entente lifted its blockade.

The change in social priorities was professionally a much easier problem to handle than the technical obstacles. The devising of new types of buildings and spatial arrangements was, then as ever, a major element of architectural skill. In pre-revolutionary Russia, social change of a different kind had been so rapid that this was a skill in constant use within the architectural profession as a whole. The middle-class apartment block, the office building and commercial headquarters, the philanthropic or cooperatively funded communal-housing block for urban industrial workers, the "people's house" (precursor of the workers' club of the twenties), the big urban secondary school for the proletariat's children, and the open institution for the higher education of workers: all were socially innovative buildings, within the Russian context, of the two decades preceding the 1917 revolution.[2]

Even that staple of Western architectural practice, the custom-made family mansion, was as new in Russia as the rich commercially based middle-class client. In the hands of someone like Moscow's great turn-of-the-century master, Fedor Shekhtel, these showpieces, planned for domestic convenience rather than classical propriety, were at least as innovative as spatial and social building types, and as aesthetically shocking to the establishment of their day as were early modernist exercises erected by the avant-garde. As part of the social statement being made by the new clients, many of these residences incorporated the very latest Western-standard environmental conveniences, experimental materials, and structural techniques (fig. 2).[3]

That, however, was before the hostilities, before the destruction and deskilling of the "ten years' sleep" in building. When El Lissitzky returned to Moscow from Germany in 1926 to publish his proposal for "skyhooks" around Moscow made of "non-rusting high-tensile steels such as are produced by Krupp" and "glass which is transparent to light but obstructs the heating rays of the sun," he might just as well have been specifying platinum and diamonds (fig. 3).[4] Public authorities were already despairing of the architectural profession's "glass mania," as more and more modernist proposals sought to bring health and light to workers by using sheets of plate glass set in bold concrete frames. And this was in a country where almost

Fig. 1. Moscow, Red Square, with Kremlin, right, looking toward St. Basil's Cathedral, ca. 1905.

no glass of any kind suitable for windows existed on the building-materials market, let alone plate.

When building resumed in the middle twenties, there was no shortage of theoretical and practical programs for dealing with these frustrations. The most interventionist were the Constructivist architects, who demanded modernized techniques for those materials they did have, notably concrete. Donkeys were still the chief power source in building work, even on prestigious Moscow sites. Cement mixers and cranes must be imported from Germany or America, they demanded, "to replace our wooden machines from the age of Leonardo da Vinci"[5] (fig. 4). Their student member Ivan Leonidov believed that the building-materials industry should be producing what architects wanted for their projects, not the other way round. With a genius for prismatically simple, essentially Suprematist spatial composition, he postulated a level of high technology in his projects that left even Lissitzky's proposals looking technically and structurally modest; in so doing, Leonidov offered powerful ammunition to the avant-garde's critics.[6]

The social priorities of the post-revolutionary years were clear and agreed upon, or at least accepted, by the architectural profession as a whole. On the other hand, the style in which such objectives should be presented, the language that would most effectively convey the revolutionary social message, was a matter of heated debate. The pluralism of today may help us understand the arguments on various sides, but the diversity in the Soviet Union of the twenties, which is so well represented in the Shchusev Museum's collection, cannot be properly described as pluralism. Pluralism signifies a democratic acceptance of diversity as the natural reflection of legitimately different political and philosophical viewpoints. Russian architectural circles of the

Fig. 2. Fedor Shekhtel, mansion for Stepan Riabushinsky, Kachalova Street, Moscow, 1900–02: detail of the garden facade. Photograph: C. Cooke.

Fig. 3. El Lissitzky, "Skyhook" project: one of the "horizontal skyscrapers," 1923. From *Izvestiia ASNOVA*, Moscow, 1926.

twenties were no more characterized by such mutual regard than Western architecture was in the heyday of modernism. In retrospect, it is interesting to note not only the arguments supporting various stylistic directions but also the terms of the case against modernism.

The latter are remarkably similar to the objections to modernism voiced fifty years later in the West: that its buildings were joylessly "industrial" in mood, ignored the cultural heritage, and therefore failed to communicate with the myths and aspirations by which the general population lived their lives.

In Russia some of these failures of communication were the result of deep differences in cultural origin between the general population and the profession and also among the architects themselves. Some were the result of a theoretical battle within Bolshevism itself over the proper source of a proletarian culture. This combination of factors produced the strange alliances that restored to prominence in the early thirties the conservative, pre-revolutionary generation of architects as executants of the aesthetic of the new dictatorship.

The architectural profession of the twenties

Within the Russian architectural profession of the twenties, we may observe the interaction between what were effectively four distinct groups. The first were middle-aged members of the pre-revolutionary profession who engaged positively with the new situation but did not substantially change their aesthetic positions. The second were those under forty, also with solid professional experience but young enough to seize the

Fig. 4. Typical Moscow building laborers laying a reinforced concrete slab, ca. 1925.

Fig. 5. Ivan Zholtovsky, mansion for industrialist Gustav Tarasov, Alexis Tolstoi Street, Moscow, 1909–12. Photograph: C. Cooke.

new theoretical challenge of post-revolutionary society, who became leaders of the main professional trends of the avant-garde. The third, whom we may call the younger leaders, completed their training just before the Revolution, benefiting from that solid background but lacking the opportunity to build. The fourth and youngest were the first student generation after the Revolution, enrolled in the "Free Studios" of the twenties, particularly in Moscow, who were taught the new curricula created by these older men, based on their various theories.

I describe this as the "Russian" rather than the "Soviet" profession advisedly because the so-called "proletarian" grouping that emerged in the late twenties to spearhead the attack on the avant-garde groups was substantially comprised of architects from other Soviet republics. Not bad modernists themselves, they were as much opposed to the professional hegemony of this Russian-rooted elite as they were to the style of their architecture.

The oldest of these four "generations" of Russian architects included practiced exponents of Classicism, eclecticism, and the Russian *art nouveau,* so-called *moderne,* before the Revolution. Firmly rooted in the social elite, they themselves constituted an artistic elite whose education at the Imperial St. Petersburg Academy or the Moscow School rivaled the best then available in the West. Most had traveled or even studied abroad. Of those whom we shall encounter as front-line professional leaders of the twenties, perhaps the most notable were Ivan Zholtovsky, Ivan Fomin, and Alexei Shchusev. The Moscow-based Zholtovsky, age fifty at the outbreak of the Revolution, was a passionate adherent of Renaissance Classicism, particularly of Palladio; he practiced widely and since 1900 had taught at the Stroganov School (fig. 5).

Fomin, forty-five, was a talented designer equally fluent in Classicism and *art nouveau.* Shchusev, forty-four, was a specialist in Russian traditional architecture and decorative arts (fig. 6).

Directly behind this generation at the time of the Revolution was a cohort of architects in their upper thirties, poised to make their mark. Among those in Petrograd was Vladimir Shchuko, age thirty-nine, who had some inventively eclectic apartment buildings to his credit. The rising stars of the profession in Moscow were the Vesnin brothers— Leonid, age thirty-seven (fig. 7), Viktor and Alexander respectively two and three years younger—who for ten years had been figuring increasingly often on the prize lists of the Moscow Architectural Society's competitions. Between the Vesnin brothers in age was Nikolai Ladovsky. The Vesnins became leaders of Constructivism in the post-revolutionary avant-garde, while Ladovsky would become leader of their rivals, the Rationalists.

A bit younger than the above men, distinct in their lack of building experience before the Revolution but subsequently contributing equally to the theory and practice of the modernist avant-garde, was a cohort born around 1890 and graduating just before the October Revolution of 1917. Backgrounds and education were more varied in this age group, but strong creative partnerships with members of the slightly older group were one of the distinctive features of the avant-garde. Here

Fig. 6. Alexei Shchusev, project for the Church of Martha and Mary convent, under the patronage of the Grand Duchess Elizabeth Fedorovna, built on Bolshaia Ordynka, Moscow, 1908–12. From *Ezhegodnik Obshchestva arkhitektorov-khudozhnikov* (Annual of the Society of Architect-Artists), no. 4, St. Petersburg, 1909, p. 135.

Fig. 7. Leonid Vesnin, project for a *dacha*. From *Ezhegodnik Moskovskago Arkhitekturnago Obshchestva* (Annual of the Moscow Architectural Society, MAO), no. 1, Moscow, 1909, p. 20.

we have Moisei Ginzburg, co-leader of Constructivism with the younger Vesnins, who finished the Riga Polytechnic in Moscow in 1917 after an earlier three-year course at the Milan Academy.

El Lissitzky's educational career had been very similar; he graduated from the Riga Polytechnic a year after Ginzburg left, after taking his first degree in Darmstadt. Vladimir Krinsky finished the Academy in Petrograd in 1917 and, like Lissitzky, became closely identified with Ladovsky in Rationalism. Konstantin Melnikov graduated from the Moscow College the same year and, like his peers, would soon be back in the reorganized schools teaching, in his case with Ilia Golosov as his older partner. Iakov Chernikhov belonged to this age group and was also soon teaching as well as studying, but a fragmented educational career put him somewhat outside the mainstream.

To a man, these new recruits to the profession in 1917 knew the old styles intimately, as their final diploma projects in school had shown. In the post-revolutionary years they would argue together fiercely over the principles that should generate a "modern" architecture, but they were united in regarding it as essentially a new phenomenon, *sui generis*, not a reinterpretation of the old canons. Within a year of the Revolution their former schools had been reorganized on freer lines by government decree, and soon they were back in these schools where, especially in Moscow, they passionately debated their new theories with colleagues from painting and literature in little "research groups," even as they taught the next generation in the studios.

Members of the generation born about 1900 were the true children of the Revolution. Their whole training, as well as their early professional experience, was conducted under the new conditions, shaped by the new social program, and limited by the new economic and technical constraints. From the Moscow VKhUTEMAS in particular—created by the amalgamation of the Moscow College and the Stroganov School to bring all two- and three-dimensional arts into one curriculum—young stars such as Ivan Leonidov, Mikhail Barshch, and Andrei Burov emerged to join Constructivism, Ivan Lamtsov, Mikhail Turkus, and Georgi Krutikov to join Rationalism, and Georgi Golts to pursue the teachings of Zholtovsky.

I stress these age differences because they help greatly in seeing behind the mass of names to the reality of the artistic and professional scene of the time, and they are fundamental to the stylistic diversity represented in the exhibition. For all the new "equalities," for all the speed with which the free debate, the frequent open competitions, and the open studio structures enabled talented newcomers to rise meteorically, the work of the leading younger architects does not emerge *ex machina*. It is the flower of inspired teaching by experienced people, deeply rooted in the aesthetic traditions of the best European and Russian architecture.

Playing against this, however, and an equally important stimulus to innovation, was undoubtedly the different cultural conditioning supplied by students innocent of most urban aesthetics, whose basic aesthetic structures were formed in rural, peasant milieus. Thus the two greatest formal innovators of the architectural avant-garde, Ivan Leonidov and Iakov Chernikhov, brought their primal, almost carnal sense of form from childhoods spent under the

Fig. 8. Sergei Maliutin, interior of the theater at Talashkino, ca. 1902, looking toward the proscenium curtain. From S. Makovsky and N. Rerich, *Talashkino: izdeliia masterskikh Kn. M K Tenishevoi* (Talashkino: products from the workshops of Princess M. K. Tenisheva), St. Petersburg, 1905, plate 150.

tough tutorship of peasant life, in constant battle with rude nature, innocent of the intellectual constructs of urbanity until well after their formative years. Melnikov, too, though singled out by a middle-class patron in adolescence, had his earliest conditioning in a similar background. These people of very different social origins fitted in with one another well enough during the melee of the twenties, although Melnikov, Leonidov, and Chernikhov retained the fiery independence that does not make easy colleagues.

The third stimulus to architectural innovation—perhaps the crucial medium of liberation—was the work of the artistic avant-garde, which far more strongly than the architectural profession had laid the foundations for its formal revolution before the political shake-up of 1917.

The new relationship between architecture and the plastic arts

In the Soviet Union of the twenties, as in Europe, the formal languages of the new architecture developed in close conjunction with—and indeed were often led by—explorations in the two- and three-dimensional areas of the fine arts. During the years when Russia was cut off from Western contact and even literature by the Civil War and the Western Entente's blockade, the Neo-plasticism of Mondrian and Vantongerloo established the formal grammars for the architecture of van Doesburg and Rietveld in Holland. Likewise in France the Purism that Corbusier and Ozenfant juxtaposed to the complex spatial structures of Cubism became the test bed for Corbusier's own essays in concrete. Social and intellectual linkages between painters and architects were, of course, a normal feature of traditional artistic culture, but the move toward abstraction in modernism generated relationships that were far more profoundly symbiotic.

Precisely because Russia immediately after the Revolution was for several years an isolated world, feeding off its own resources while the Bolsheviks gradually extended their conquests, and Western powers tried to cut their supply lines, the internal conjuncture gave unique coloration to artistic developments. Internal intellectual battles and alliances were being worked through within the larger revolutionary process, and many cultural shifts that paralleled Western developments, or others that represented belated cultural modernization, were propagated with passionately political and ideological rationales.

The traditional relationship between art and architecture operated in pre-revolutionary Russia as in the West, whether in Classicist circles around the Imperial Academy in Petersburg or in the Slavophile movement that protested against it in the later nineteenth century. This relationship was strengthened in the influential arts-and-crafts colonies of rich patrons like Savva Mamontov or Princess Tenisheva at Abramtsevo and Talashkino respectively (fig. 8)[7]. Here mutual learning could take place across the conventional boundaries of artistic and craft disciplines, and activity flowed naturally into theater, opera, and fine art publishing. Both of these patrons financed such ventures as Sergei Diaghilev and Alexander Benois's journal *World of Art*.[8] Firmly rooted in the Abramtsevo colony, for example, was the most important artistic confraternity in turn-of-the-century Moscow, which linked the *art nouveau* architect Fedor Shekhtel, writer Anton Chekhov, theater director Konstantin Stanislavsky, and the Symbolist painter, sculptor, and ceramicist Mikhail Vrubel.[9]

In its own context this was a genuine spiritual and aesthetic symbiosis, but it was naturally anathema to those excluded from such cultural elites. The boundaries were not just social. They were reinforced by blinkered teaching even in the relatively freer schools like the Moscow College (from which Tatlin had been dismissed for lack of aptitude) and by a very exclusive exhibitions policy in the established galleries (on which Tatlin had expressed himself in the press, as well as to Benois just before the First World War).[10]

At that stage Tatlin was a young painter who had been to Paris, had seen Picasso's three-dimensional collages, and was now producing assemblages from

Fig. 9. Vladimir Tatlin, *Hanging Corner Relief,* selection of materials, iron, aluminium, and primer, 1915. From N. Punin, *Tatlin: protiv kubizma* (Tatlin: against Cubism), Petersburg (Petrograd), 1921.

bits of timber and metal which he called "counter-reliefs" or "selections of materials" (fig. 9). His principal concern, in the improvised alternative art shows of Moscow and Petrograd, was to outshine his older rival Kazimir Malevich as innovative guru within their newly abstractionist avant-garde circle. Malevich's innovations were, of course, entirely different in media and philosophical intention. Where Tatlin declared his new subject matter to be the interaction of "real materials in real space," Malevich's concern, in his painted Suprematist canvases, was to create a new system of painterly forms that communicated the sensation of pure energy and force in the cosmic space that "is within my own skull" (fig. 10). Tatlin did not say much. Malevich addressed his public and colleagues in long, philosophical, and poetic ramblings. But between them, this extraordinary pair of talents created the two foundations, even the two formal and spatial languages, from which avant-garde architecture (quite apart from much else) would build most of its radical propositions.[11]

By 1920 the thirty-five-year-old Tatlin was no longer just the young sailor-painter with a police record for "revolutionary views." After the Revolution he had become a major figure in the new official artistic and cultural hierarchy set up by Lenin's art and culture commissar, Anatoly Lunacharsky. Tatlin now had the chance to spit at the pre-revolutionary establishment he had so despised, and to powerful ideological effect. In a statement on his *Monument to the Third International,* he said that before the Revolution "all foundations on which the plastic arts stood were at odds with each other, and all the connections linking painting with sculpture and architecture had been lost. The result was individualism, i.e., the expression of merely personal habits and tastes. When artists addressed material, they reduced it to the level of

Fig. 10. Kazimir Malevich, *Airplane Flying*, 1915. The Museum of Modern Art, New York. Purchase.

something they could do eccentric things with vis-à-vis one or other branch of fine art. So at best the artist decorated the walls of private mansions—of individual nests."[12]

Referring to one of Fedor Shekhtel's masterpieces in Moscow, richly decorated with thematic ceramics from the Abramtsevo studios and paintings by the great Konstantin Korovin, Tatlin mocked that artistic fraternity for "leaving us a series of 'Iaroslavl railway stations' (fig. 11) and a multitude of other forms that now seem comical." While the Revolution had discredited this work, it had merely effected a social catching-up process in relation to his own, which had "already taken material, volume and construction" as its very subject matter back in 1914. "The purely artistic forms" resulting from that "research into material, volume and construction" represented, said Tatlin, "laboratory models" for the solution of "utilitarian tasks" posed now, after the Revolution, "in our task of creating a new world."[13] Suitably entitled "The work ahead of us," this statement encapsulated the crucial idea of the new relationship between the different scales of plastic art, integral rather than accidental, and effectively set the agenda for the whole modernist avant-garde.

Among the artistic avant-garde in Russia after the Revolution it thus became a central principle that the proper function of those practices and crafts previously called "fine arts," addressed to a bourgeois market, now lay in formal research for the larger spatial constructions required by the masses of the socialist society, that is, for buildings, urbanism, and the organization of the whole environment.[14] Precisely

Fig. 11. Fedor Shekhtel, Iaroslavl Station, Moscow, 1902, drawing of main elevation. From E. Kirichenko, *Fedor Shekhtel*, Moscow, 1973.

such an idea underpinned Lissitzky's concept of the "Proun" as the "interchange station between painting and architecture."[15] Following on from Tatlin, the Constructivist architects described their research into formal and spatial configurations as "laboratory work" for full-scale architecture. Alexander Rodchenko, who carried forward the thrust of Tatlin's ideas among the younger Moscow artists, would talk of his little assemblages of wooden blocks as elements of a "spatial inventory" for application in larger functional tasks.[16] Malevich moved into the three-dimensional world of his *arkhitektoniki* with a similar intention (fig. 12). This principle became the basis of their teaching in the new schools, as well as of their own practice. To such an extent did this view become an orthodoxy across the whole spectrum of aesthetic creeds in the early twenties that leading avant-garde artists who uncompromisingly insisted on art's unique function as the reflective spiritual essay left Russia for the bourgeois West while they could. The most conspicuous to go were Vasily Kandinsky and Naum Gabo.[17]

Much of the fecundity of the modernist architectural avant-garde in Russia derives from its dual origins in these two groups, from the cross-fertilization between the vigorous new generations in the architectural profession and its explosively creative peer group within the other plastic arts. Certain alliances had already been formed across this interprofessional divide among the younger members before the Revolution, most notably the close friendship between Tatlin and Alexander Vesnin. In general, however, it was the common tasks in the immediate post-revolutionary years that threw them together.

Revolutionary engagement

Faced with enormous distances, a politically immature and mainly illiterate population, the victorious Bolsheviks faced real problems in communicating to the still unreliable masses the nature of the new regime and the battle that had been fought. They engaged artists of various persuasions who would collaborate, using all the visual and symbolic media that were available. Sometimes the results were highly innovative; sometimes they were no more than a change of content in a form that was culturally well established.

The Russian Orthodox Church had for centuries forbidden the making of human images, so it was traditional to erect buildings rather than statues as monuments to great victories. Thus some of the very first building designs after the Revolution were actually projects for "monuments" advertising the fact of the political takeover. In the major cities, particularly Moscow and Petrograd, traditional mass street fairs for Shrovetide and Imperial coronations were reworked into a new medium: the revolutionary festival. City squares were decorated with ideological symbols and slogans, and workers' groups paraded with floats mocking Tsarist counter-revolutionaries, capitalists, and leaders of the hostile Entente powers. (Today's May Day and November 7 parades are the continuation of this.)[18]

The two earliest works in the exhibition exemplify the enthusiastic contributions of younger architects to these two genres of political consolidation immediately after the Revolution. It is unclear why a competition took place in 1917 for "a monument to revolutionary heroes in Helsingfors" (Helsinki). (Finland used the Revolution as its opportunity to get free of Russian domination.) But Vladimir Shchuko's extraordinary triumphal arch, half Classical, half Egyptian, is a typical Russian "monument" of that genre (plate 1). Its heavy monumentality was characteristic of many such projects of the early twenties. Nikolai Kolli was a Moscow architecture student who had worked for Shchusev, among others, before the Revolution delayed completion of his studies. The talent that would later, as a young Constructivist, make

him Corbusier's executive architect for the Tsentrosoyuz complex in Moscow[19] is already displayed in the splendid "monument" he designed and built just off Red Square for the street festival celebrating the first anniversary of the Revolution (plate 2; see also fig. 13). Lest any workers should fail to understand the symbolism, the white block of the executed project was clearly labeled "Bands of White Guardsmen" (Tsarist loyalists) across the crack created by the Red Wedge of Bolsheviks. (Lissitzky's famous poster on a similar theme dates from the following year.)[20]

During the regime's first year, a network of arts administrations called IZO was set up by Anatoly Lunacharsky's Commissariat of Enlightenment, Narkompros. IZO became a meeting ground for all generations.[21] In Moscow, for example, figures as different in age and culture as Zholtovsky and Tatlin played leading roles from the beginning. When ambitious city architectural and planning bureaus were established in 1919 in Moscow and Petrograd, Lunacharsky personally recommended Zholtovsky to Lenin as head of the Moscow bureau on the basis of his proven commitment to IZO. "Although keeping out of politics and not a Party member, he has proved his loyalty to our Soviet regime," Lunacharsky wrote.[22] Soon Zholtovsky was joined by Shchusev, and they assembled an office of young architects whose work had attracted their attention before the Revolution. Among them were Konstantin Melnikov, Nikolai Ladovsky, Nikolai Kolli, Ilia Golosov, and Leonid Vesnin. In Petrograd, Vladimir Shchuko was appointed to lead IZO's architectural activity, and Ivan Fomin headed the planning bureau, with elder

Fig. 12. Kazimir Malevich, *Arkhitektoniki,* mid-1920s.

statesmen like Alexander Benois as consultants. In Moscow particularly, under Zholtovsky, the city planning bureau became the kind of public office that is a focus for open discussions as lively as in any teaching studio, where bright young architects could quickly gain confidence in their own potential. As these names indicate, the office was an important launchpad for the architectural avant-garde.[23]

While Malevich went to Vitebsk and formed his UNOVIS group (Affirmers of the New Art) in the art school there with Lissitzky, Tatlin was running artistic and cultural affairs for IZO in Moscow and developing his famous contribution to the tradition of "buildings as monuments"—his *Monument to the Third International* (fig. 14). Seeking easier working conditions, he went to Petrograd to build the model. Meanwhile, in Moscow young architects and abstract artists made a first attempt to come together across the old professional divide in a group they called Paint-Sculpt-Arch: Zhivskulptarkh.[24] The resulting architectural "investigations" showed the role played by Cubism in building a first bridge across the professional divide toward an architecture that rejected not just the formal languages of traditional building but the very notion of stability on which they rested. The typically utopian theme dominating their explorations was a Temple of Communion between Nations, for which Ladovsky's young supporter Vladimir Krinsky contributed several ideas[25] (plates 6 and 7).

Probably under the influence of their painter colleagues in Inkhuk (the Institute of Artistic Culture in Moscow), which replaced Zhivskulptarkh with a speed characteristic of those unstable years, the language became more planar and more clearly structured. Thus Krinsky's works from 1920 (plates 3 and 4) are closer to the contemporaneous work of artists like Liubov Popova or Alexander Rodchenko, with whom for a while they converged.[26] The next year, 1921, saw them part again when experimentation and debate had clarified in their minds how the new notion of "construction," derived ultimately from the inspiration of Tatlin, differed as an aesthetic principle from the traditional notion of "composition." "Construction," many believed, crucially embodied the spirit and philosophical essence of the age, and of their new world in particular. Each had taken his own stance on the role these "constructive principles" should play in his future work within the new ideology.[27] These debates were to be a watershed in the development of

Fig. 13.   V. I. Lenin speaks from the tribune in Red Square on the first anniversary of the Revolution, November 7, 1918. From a memorial volume, *Lenin 1870–1924*, Moscow–Leningrad, 1939.

Fig. 14. Vladimir Tatlin, *Monument to the Third International,* model in studio, 1919. From N. Punin, *Tatlin: protiv kubizma* (Tatlin: against Cubism), Petersburg (Petrograd), 1921.

avant-garde architecture, as the two camps that formed—the adherents of "construction" and of "composition"—contained the embryos of the Constructivist and Rationalist groups in architecture.

The topics of this early work by future Rationalist leaders Ladovsky and Krinsky begin to reflect the new social circumstances. There is a festival bridge decoration celebrating the Communist International from Krinsky (plate 19), and Ladovsky contributes a scaled section of his communal-housing project (plates 10 and 11). But the point was made with a Krinsky work (plate 8), which prefaced The Museum of Modern Art's 1988 exhibition "Deconstructivist Architecture," that the structural references here are determinedly anti-constructive. With a Civil War raging around them, economic stasis, and the building industry reduced to a tabula rasa, who could say where "realism" in construction lay?

It is clear from this group of works that expressive potential is the focus of interest. Generally the expressive medium is form, but some items, such as Krinsky's bright gridded "structure in space" (plate 26), represent the supplementary importance accorded to color by the painters in this group. When the VKhUTEMAS school was created in Moscow in late 1920, the members of Inkhuk took over the crucial basic or foundation course, akin to the Bauhaus *Vorkurs,* which was the common preparation for students of all artistic and design disciplines.[28] The collection of schoolwork by the student Ivan Lamtsov (plates 12–15, 18), completed under the direct tutelage of Ladovsky in 1921–22, shows the full range of set exercises, from those devoted purely to the formal expression of such sensations as weight and mass to first extensions of this work in the direction of making "buildings." Lidia Komarova's responses to the same exercises a year later (plates 16 and 17) make an interesting comparison; where Lamtsov remained with Ladovsky and Krinsky in Rationalism, Komarova would end up with Vesnin and Ginzburg in Constructivism.[29]

As these two doctrines crystallized in the early twenties, another area of artistic work—the theater—played an important part in the development of a new architectural language, in addition to providing gentle propaganda for the revolutionary cause. Here, too, the early Soviet work built upon an area of Russian cultural life that had been particularly vigorous before the war, where participation of the most progressive painters and architects was a normal result of the synthetic aspirations of such pre-revolutionary movements as Symbolism and the World of Art group. Just as Vasnetsov and Korovin had led the way from Abramtsevo, and Benois with Diaghilev, so Shekhtel, Shchuko, and Alexander Vesnin had followed. After the Revolution, young emerging Constructivists such as Vesnin's companion, Liubov Popova, and Rodchenko's wife, Varvara Stepanova—as yet unable to design the useful furniture or buildings to which they aspired—extended their artistic experiments in "constructing" things to frameworks, stage equipment, and abstract costumes for the dynamic productions of new-wave producers like Vsevolod Meyerhold.[30]

Typical of these collaborations of the early twenties, the play itself was bourgeois, and only the interpretation was "revolutionary." For producer Alexander Tairov's 1923 presentation of G. K. Chesterton's *The Man Who Was Thursday,* Alexander Vesnin created a mechanized Western metropolis that remained the avant-garde vision of the future city. The actors hated the structure for slowing rather than speeding their action, but this marvelous collection of Vesnin's sketches (plates 30–34) provides a unique close-up of what some of the avant-garde's architectural projects might have looked like had they been built. Indeed that same year the first invitations to think larger—even modestly to build—were emerging.

As the twenties progressed, Soviet society's efforts to restructure its public organizations as well as everyday life led to widespread demand for new building types. Architectural competitions became one of the main stimuli and showcases for innovation in these areas. The professional organization that oversaw most of the competitions was the Moscow Architectural Society (MAO). Through war and revolution the now elderly Shekhtel had remained its president, but as the new world came to life, Shchusev replaced him in 1922. That autumn MAO announced the first major competition for a state building of the new regime: a Palace of Labor, or workers' parliament, to stand just north of Red Square. It was to celebrate the creation of a new unified state, the USSR, after the end of the Civil War and, in Stalin's words as Party secretary, "the triumph of the new Russia over the old." It must show the West, said another Party leader, Sergei Kirov, "that we are capable of adorning this sinful earth with such works of great architecture as our enemies never dreamed of."[31] Ladovsky and his colleagues refused to enter the competition, though some did projects privately. They reckoned that a jury composed of Shekhtel, Zholtovsky, and the *World of Art* critic Igor Grabar would make it a waste of their time.

Faced with a brief that called for enormous auditoriums and accommodation, and the revolutionary monumentality obviously expected, most of the entries could be described as "bulbous expressionism." It was indeed a tamed version of that genre by a Petrograder, Noi Trotsky, that won. Here we have two interestingly contrasted schemes: a rather well-articulated example of that type by Andrei Belogrud of Petrograd (plates 35 and 36), who had become rector of the Academy School when it re-formed from the "Free Studios" in 1921,[32] and the Vesnin brothers' entry, which got third prize (plates 37–41). Applauding the latter's "attempt to create a new social organism, whose life flowed not from stereotypes of the past but from the novelty of the brief itself," and the "simple, logical three-dimensional expression" of that externally, Moisei Ginzburg would later describe the Vesnins' project as "the first demonstration of our new approach" and "the first concrete architectural action of Constructivism."[33]

As part of the campaign to revive small-scale industry and trade under Lenin's New Economic Policy, a major Agricultural and Handicraft Industries Exhibition was held in Moscow in the summer of 1923 on the riverside site of today's Gorky Park. It was everyone's first chance to build something and therefore generated enormous enthusiasm and interesting collaborations. Shchusev and Zholtovsky did overall planning and supervision, although young students such as Kolli and Andrei Burov, as well as the older Golosov brother, Panteleimon, took prizes in a competition for some aspects of the layout. Zholtovsky's main official pavilions showed that even the cheapest timber could not upset his talent for harmonious proportions and classical ordering (fig. 15). One of his pavilions had "constructive" relief decoration by the young artists Alexandra Exter and the Stenberg brothers. Elsewhere Popova

and Rodchenko contributed, while Shekhtel did the pavilion for Turkestan in the non-Russian section, and Ilia Golosov designed the playful, spatially quite complex little quadrant-shaped building of the Far Eastern republics (plate 22). Shchuko from Petrograd did the foreign section, including a boldly modernist restaurant complex (fig. 16).[34] The published records do not make clear whether such student designs as Georgi Golts's little bandstand (plate 23) or Lamtsov's bottle-shaped beer kiosk (plate 24) ever were built, but the drawings convey the exuberance of the exhibition as a designers' event. For the development of avant-garde architecture, the most important building was Melnikov's pavilion for the state tobacco trust, Makhorka (fig. 17). He later described it as his "best ever building,"[35] which one might question, but its dynamic volumes caused a sensation and were a steppingstone to his next exhibition pavilion, for Paris in 1925.

The year 1924 was a frenzied one for competitions. Monuments remained in demand, and Fomin's design for a memorial to the revolutionary leader Sverdlov exemplifies a continuing type of inventive but still classically based monumentality that characterized much architecture at this time. Lenin's death in January of that year caused the revolutionary city of Petrograd to be renamed Leningrad and heralded a spate of competitions for memorials and buildings named for Lenin in major towns all over the USSR. Among the competition projects for a Lenin House of the People in the textile city of Ivanovo-Voznesensk was one by Ilia Golosov (plate 50). The great leader's first temporary mausoleum on Red Square was a modest wooden structure by Shchusev, quickly replaced by a second temporary version, also wooden, where Lenin's embalmed body lay under

Fig. 15. Ivan Zholtovsky with Nikolai Kolli et al. Courtyard view of the Machine Building Pavilion at the All-Russian Agricultural and Handicraft Industries Exhibition, Moscow, 1923. From M. Ginzburg, *Stil i epokha* (Style and Epoch), Moscow, 1924, plate 3.

a glazed sarcophagus by Melnikov.[36] Under the chairmanship of Lunacharsky, the Commission for a Permanent Mausoleum for Lenin then launched a multi-stage competition for a masonry building that would "fit into the architecture of the Square."[37] The main reason for the competition boom, however, was the revival of the economy to a point where new building might again be contemplated. The outburst of design activity by the young avant-garde in response to the rising crescendo of competitions reflected the growing maturity of a self-confident new generation of architects.

A competition was held to design modest Moscow headquarters for the Party

newspaper *Leningrad Pravda* on a site only 6m by 6m, located on what is today Pushkin Square. The challenge of such compactness and the requirement for "an expression of the building's agitational character"[38] produced three wonderfully inventive and dynamic solutions from the emerging stars of the avant-garde: Melnikov, the Vesnin brothers, and Ilia Golosov. Melnikov, the youngest designer, produced a typically quirky scheme (plate 46). Around a central core of vertical circulation, six lozenge-shaped volumes would rotate independently to produce a constantly changing silhouette. Perhaps more than any other design by Melnikov, it shows the influence of Tatlin and the dream of high technology. Golosov's building used more conventional architectural means to achieve its dynamism, with faceted elevations produced by the complex star-shaped floor plans, the shifting staircase routes inside, and diagonal bands of graphics that follow them externally. The Vesnins' project (plate 47) has external elevators and exudes an enjoyment of movement that refers more to Alexander's theatrical structures than to Tatlin in its exploitation of the constructive pleasure of the simple trabeated frame. Two years later when their followers had formed a Constructivist architectural group and launched a magazine, it was no surprise to find this Vesnin project featured on the first page as a canonical work.[39]

In its modest size the project had the professional buildability that was beginning to be the Vesnins' hallmark and key to success. It got them first prize in another important Moscow competition that year—for the headquarters of the Anglo-Russian trading partnership, ARCOS, a complex of offices, hotel, restaurant, and retail shops on a site in the city's old banking and commercial district east of Red Square.[40] Theirs was a highly professional bit of planning in a frame structure (fig. 18), and the two competing schemes in the exhibition

Fig. 16. Vladimir Shchuko, café-restaurant in the foreign section of the All-Russian Agricultural and Handicraft Industries Exhibition, Moscow, 1923. From M. Ginzburg, *Stil i epokha* (Style and Epoch), Moscow, 1924, plate 6.

Fig. 17. Konstantin Melnikov, Pavilion for the Makhorka tobacco trust, All-Russian Agricultural and Handicraft Industries Exhibition, Moscow, 1923. From M. Ginzburg, *Stil i epokha* (Style and Epoch), Moscow, 1924, plate 18.

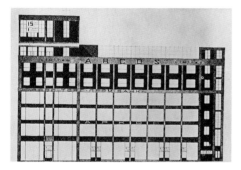

Fig. 18. Leonid, Alexander, and Viktor Vesnin, project for the Anglo-Russian Trading Company (ARCOS), Moscow, 1924. From M. Ginzburg, *Style and Epoch*, translated by A. Senkevitch (Cambridge, Mass.: Oppositions/MIT Press, 1982), plate 14.

show how far ahead of their rivals the Vesnin brothers were at this stage in approaching Western standards of professionalism, combining solid pre-revolutionary experience with the vigor of the new aesthetic interest in structure among their artist friends. Young Krinsky's framed building (plate 44) is a mere diagram by comparison. The scheme by young Leningrader Alexander Gegello (plates 42 and 43) pursues a different line. His giant order of four-storied bay windows is still redolent of the romantic Classicism that dominated Petrograd architecture just after the Revolution. At the same time it already presages something of the attempt to match Classicism to the grids of a concrete frame which his teacher Fomin would soon be pursuing more rigorously into a theory of Proletarian Classicism.

Gegello was only four years out of college but would soon be playing an important role in Leningrad modernism. His first practical contribution would be made in workers' housing (plate 62), where the strong garden-city tradition of Petersburg produced some attractive low-rise work.

1925: Modernist or Classical?

In terms of prestige, the most important competition of 1924 was that for the Soviet pavilion for the next year's Exposition des Arts Décoratifs in Paris—the first occasion for the new Soviet state to present itself on an international stage with a specially designed building. Lunacharsky, who was aware of the quality of the design work being done in the schools, particularly the VKhUTEMAS, as well as by designers such as Rodchenko and Popova and also in the theater, coopted the artist and poet Vladimir Mayakovsky to advise on interior display. A closed competition was launched for a building that would "express the idea of the USSR and distinguish itself from the usual European architecture."[41] The Muscovites invited were all modernists representing the three main strands in the city: the

Vesnins (who did not submit), Ginzburg, Krinsky, Ladovsky, their colleague Nikolai Dokuchaev, Ilia Golosov, and Melnikov; the Leningraders were Shchuko and Fomin. Melnikov took the prize with the famous timber and glass building (fig. 19) that created a sensation and put the new Soviet architecture on the world map. (Drawings for this project are in the family collection.[42]) Here, as with the ARCOS competition, we have the drawings for two highly contrasting projects, one each from Leningrad and Moscow, that well reflect the different states of architecture in the two cities at this date. Even better do they reflect the two approaches to design around which architecture would polarize at the end of the decade.

Golosov's scheme (plate 49) is vigorous modernism from the hand of a naturally talented designer. It lacks the clarity of a single overriding idea that was always Melnikov's trademark—indeed the key to his design approach—but in this context, as in the Agricultural Exhibition, Golosov's touches of playfulness, like his strong color, are entirely appropriate for an exhibition building.

Fomin's starting point was equally the determination "to make a new style," but it would be one that "does not have recourse to the affectations and ultra-futuristic approaches which are difficult to actually build, and are too flashy." As he explained:

I have been concerned above all that the style of the pavilion should reflect the character of the workers' and peasants' government of this country. Therefore my architecture has a somewhat utilitarian character and combines decorative elements appropriate to exhibitions with elements of industrial and factory building, as is clear from the perspective drawing [plate 48]. The central figure is a worker, calling others, and on all sides the architectural forms gravitate toward him, as a symbol of

Fig. 19. Konstantin Melnikov, Pavilion of the
USSR, Exposition des Arts Décoratifs, Paris,
1925, entrance. Courtesy A. Kopp.

*how all nationalities are aspiring to
unite in response to the call of the
worker and have come together into the
USSR.*[43]

This project and Fomin's description are
highly interesting as an early example
of the aesthetic rationale that would
form the basis of Socialist Realism at
the end of the decade. It, too, would seek
a new symbolism, rooted in the population's own situation and the reality of
current politics, through a synthesis of
modern building technologies with
representational elements readily under-
stood by the people. By the time of the
great architectural competitions of the
early thirties, the power balance had
moved far enough in the direction of
centralism and a new autocracy of the
Party for the supposedly democratic elements of this pronouncement to sound a
false note. But in 1924 it still rang true.
The problem, however, which was central to the dilemma of the twenties,
concerned the audience: to whom was
the architecture being addressed?

The decision to use Melnikov's design
for Paris is said to have been influenced
significantly by its obvious buildability
and value for money. These factors, combined with its dramatic formal
simplicity and lack of decorative rhetoric, are what attracted public and
professional attention in Paris in the
midst of the various Art Deco styles of
the rest of the exhibition. But those very
features, which were increasingly developed by the avant-garde in the next few
years, made it certain that "the new
architecture" would never gain easy
acceptance at home in the Soviet Union.
The roots of this situation lay deep
within the thinking of the Party.

Since before the Revolution, two views
on the proper starting point for a proletarian art and culture had competed
for support among Bolshevik Party the-
orists. The view particularly associated

with the organization called Proletkult and its leader, Alexander Bogdanov, insisted that the past be treated essentially as a tabula rasa, on which proletarian culture was to be built as a new structure based on new principles. Opposed to this was Lenin's view that the proletariat's culture, like its technology, must build positively but critically upon the achievements of its predecessor, capitalism.[44] The newly invented "abstract systems," which he tended to sum up as "futurism," were bourgeois distractions and positively harmful. In Lenin's own words of 1920:

Proletarian culture is not something dreamed up out of nowhere; nor is it the invention of people who call themselves specialists in proletarian culture. That is all complete nonsense. Proletarian culture must emerge from the steady development of those reserves of experience which humanity has built up under the yoke of capitalism.[45]

As Marx had said, "Everything that was created by humanity before us" must be critically assessed, and "the treasures of art and science must be made accessible to the whole popular mass."[46] It is immediately clear why the stripped modernism of the avant-garde might be criticized as "anti-Leninist."

It is equally clear why the old guard of the architectural profession should prove useful, as the common feature of those whom I identified as "the over-forties of 1917" was precisely the conviction that something of continuing (perhaps even eternal) validity lay in Classicism. To Zholtovsky, it rested in the absolutes of Renaissance proportional systems, in particular those of Palladio. His teaching during the twenties was particularly directed at the refinement of proportional systems in industrial architecture.[47] Ivan Fomin was credited with being the first, before the Revolution, to identify Classicism as just as "national" to Russia as her medieval tradition.[48] In his reworking of that tradition for the new context,

specific proportional systems were not significant. It was the parallel between the post-and-lintel structure of Classicism and the "democratic" concrete frame which he used to produce his stripped and stretched "order" of Proletarian Classicism.[49] To Shchusev, Classicism and Russian medieval architecture represented a standard of sophistication and embellishment to which everything with pretensions to being "architecture" must aspire, to be relinquished only so far as poverty of means might temporarily dictate.[50] To Shchuko and Zholtovsky, proportions were the essence of architecture, but no single source had a monopoly on "correctness"; clarity of monumental massing was an equal criterion of architectural value.[51] However apolitical the views of these people, their cultural conservatism made them more useful to the architectural program of Leninism than the politically engagé modernists who were trying to create something new. Adulation of "the new Soviet architecture" from the Paris intelligentsia was thus an unreliable guide to its relevance at home. Back in 1920, Lunacharsky had stressed the non-transferability of modernism across cultural boundaries:

Within the line of development of European art, Impressionism, all forms of Neo-Impressionism, Cubism, Futurism and Suprematism are natural phenomena.... All this work, entirely conscientious and important as it is, has the character of laboratory research.... But the proletariat and the more cultivated sections of the peasantry did not live through any of the stages of European or Russian art, and they are at an entirely different stage of development.[52]

If not that, what? The answer came in Lunacharsky's speech to the Communist International a year later:

The proletariat will also continue the art of the past, but will begin from some healthy stage, like the Renaissance.... If we are talking of the masses, the natural form of their art will be the traditional and classical one, clear to the point of transparency, resting ... on healthy, convincing realism and on eloquent, transparent symbolism in decorative and monumental forms.[53]

The lesson is clear: Melnikov might be well-judged material for the bourgeois eye of Paris, but Fomin's scheme was a more relevant model for responding to the cultural condition in the USSR itself.

Alternative theories of modernism

After an agreeable sojourn in the Paris spotlight with Mayakovsky and Rodchenko, Melnikov returned to Moscow to build the series of workers' clubs and the personal house which consolidated his place in the profession over the next few years. Increasingly he was a lone figure as a result of his individualistic approach to design as well as his presumption that the Paris project had earned him a prestige status in Moscow. The year 1925–26 represents a useful datum in the development of the avant-garde. The takeoff in building reinforced the already polarizing attitudes as to what the new architecture should be, with the state's economic and aesthetic policies seeming to pull architecture in opposite directions. At its 14th Party Congress in December 1925, the Soviet government finally decided in favor of an industry-led rather than an agriculture-led strategy for development and reconstruction of the economy. Production was back to the levels from which it had collapsed at the outbreak of the First World War; the peasantry were proving recalcitrant, and a series of campaigns were launched presenting rationalization and mechanization as the keys to Soviet economic advancement.

In architecture the only formally constituted new group to have emerged since the Revolution was the Association of New Architects (ASNOVA), which had been formed by Ladovsky and Krinsky in 1923 when they first began to develop a philosophy of architecture based on the science of visual perception.[54] They called themselves Rationalists, and Ladovsky explained that "architectural rationalism stands for economy of psychic energy in the perception of spatial and functional aspects of a building."[55] He contrasted this to "technical rationalism," whose priority is the economy of materials. The basis of their design teaching remained unchanged from what it had been back in the days of Zhivskulptarkh in 1919:

In planning any given building, the architect must first of all assemble and compose only space, not concerning himself with material and construction.... Construction enters into architecture only in so far as it determines a concept of space. The engineer's basic principle is to invest the minimum amount of material to obtain maximum results. This has nothing in common with art and can only serve the requirements of architecture incidentally.[56]

In 1926 Ladovsky published as his "Foundations for building a theory of architecture" a statement first made in late 1920, explaining that the function of design was to create " 'motifs,' which in architectural terms must be 'rational,' and must serve the higher technical requirement of the individual, *to orientate himself in space*"[57] (the emphasis is his own). By 1925–26 this was the basis of their teaching in both architecture and planning. They had a research program under way in "psychotechnics," basing their empirical research on work done at Harvard by the German emigré Hugo Munsterberg, and they hoped to set up a laboratory for their strange apparatuses in the VKhUTEMAS (fig. 20).[58]

Fig. 20. Nikolai Ladovsky, equipment in his psychotechnical laboratory, ca. 1927. From *Stroitel'stvo Moskvy* (Construction of Moscow), 1928, no. 10, p. 17.

In early 1926 the Rationalists were still claiming that this work "must have great practical importance in everyday architectural practice,"[59] but the supporters of Vesnin and Rodchenko, with their interest in real construction as a principle, disagreed strongly enough to form a rival architectural group. Thus in the last days of December 1925 the Union of Contemporary Architects (OSA) was created under the leadership of the Vesnins and Ginzburg. All were colleagues intellectually of the Constructivist artists and designers associated with Mayakovsky, Rodchenko, and the literary group called LEF.[60]

Corbusier had been a point of reference for these architects (fig. 21) since his writing in *L'Esprit Nouveau* first filtered into Russia in 1922 when he sent some copies to Lunacharsky. It was one of the stimuli and reference points for Ginzburg's "manifesto" of Constructivist architecture, *Style and Epoch,* published in 1924.[61] In his theory of historical stylistic development, as well as his analysis of the machine's relevance as a design model, Ginzburg had unquestionably moved beyond the relatively facile and highly selective stance of Corbusier. And in a holiday letter to his brothers in the summer of 1924, Leonid Vesnin commented on his rereading of the lately published *Vers une architecture:* "I am reading Corbusier-Saugnier but fairly slowly, and therefore more carefully than I did last winter. I see that there are certain questions on which one could already disagree with him. We have gone further and we look more deeply."[62]

Apart from properties of spatial and technical economy, the functional ordering of movement, and clear, essentially additive formal "construction," what the Constructivists took from the engineer was the rationality, as they saw it, of his method of designing. As Ginzburg wrote

under the title "New methods of architectural thinking" in the lead article of the very first issue of their journal, *Contemporary Architecture,* "The social conditions of our contemporary world are such" that the problem of "individual aesthetic preferences" has given way to that of generating "rational new types in architecture." Inclusion of the architect within the overall production chain of the country meant the end of that "isolation which previously existed between various forms of architectural and engineering activity."[63]

With a reference perhaps to Tatlin, he wrote: "Certainly it would be naive to replace the complex art of architecture by an imitation of even the most

Fig. 21. Leonid Vesnin, Le Corbusier, Alexander Vesnin, Andrei Burov (front, left to right), and other Constructivists in Alexander Vesnin's apartment, with one of his paintings in the background, Moscow, 1928. From A. G. Chiniakov, *Bratia Vesniny* (The Vesnin Brothers), Moscow, 1970, p. 14.

sparkling forms of contemporary technology. This period of naive 'machine symbolism' is already outdated. In this field *it is only the inventor's creative method that the contemporary architect must master.*"

Whatever the building type, Ginzburg continued, the architect should adopt the same approach, "proceeding from the main questions to the secondary ones ... in a logical ordering of all the factors impinging on the task," which are equally social, environmental, and constructional. "The result will be a spatial solution which, like any other kind of rationally generated organism, is divided into individual organs that have been developed in response to the functional roles which each one fulfills." The first architectural result—and this is very evident in their work, as in much modernism—"is a new type of plan. These contemporary plans are generally asymmetrical, since it is extremely rare for functions to be identical. They are predominantly open and free in their configurations, because this not only bathes each part of the building in fresh air and sunlight, but makes its functional elements more clearly readable and makes it easier to perceive the dynamic life that is unfolding within the building's spaces."[64]

The Constructivists' so-called "functional method," developed in some detail in their writings, was thus an essentially linear ordering of design considerations, "each one building logically upon the other," as Ginzburg said, and ending with considerations of aesthetic refinement in detail and overall massing.[65] In this latter category their method subsumed the concerns of ASNOVA, but, as is clear here, it was enormously wider. Aesthetically many of their earlier projects, as we have seen with the Vesnin competition work, were very strong expressions of a frame that

sometimes hinted at steel but usually employed vast areas of glass. Another example of this group is the Vesnins' design for the Mostorg department store built in Moscow's Krasnaia Presnia district in 1927 (plate 52). Later, with concrete and rendered blockwork becoming the technical norm for their "economic structures," the work generally follows the stylistic model offered for such technology by Corbusier. A very typical example is the Vesnins' headquarters building for the Ivanovo-Voznesensk agricultural bank, Ivselbank (plate 53), also erected in 1927. Both buildings were conceived as accessible, proletarian versions of the corresponding bourgeois types.

Even as the Constructivists were consolidating their group and building the elements of a new urbanism around these lessons of engineering and the machine, the unacceptability of this model was being forcefully stressed by Lunacharsky in a speech of autumn 1926 to the State Academy of Artistic Sciences (GAKhN) in Moscow. For all the noisy state propaganda campaigns that were currently presenting maximum mechanization as the key to Soviet economic advancement, Lunacharsky declared:

Let the rhythm of the machine certainly become some element of our culture, but the machine cannot become the center of our art ... because it can only push the proletariat towards individualism.... It is only the bourgeoisie that can limit itself to urbanism [as the generator of its creative work]—only futurism and the artists of LEF.[66]

These, of course, were the Constructivists. Infatuation with the machine, Lunacharsky said, "is the cry of leftist urbanism of Euro-American culture," whereas the basis of proletarian creativity should be "vernacular, peasant art . . . because of the collective principles underlying its products."[67] The writing was certainly on the wall.

If these were the theoretical positions and design approaches of the two main avant-garde groups in architecture, the Rationalists and the Constructivists, what of those leading modernist architects unrelated or peripheral to them?

Melnikov, the most conspicuous example, was not naturally attracted to any theories or groups. Before his career took off in a different direction with the success of his Paris pavilion and Moscow clubs, he had some informal links with ASNOVA. Both he and Ilia Golosov had been at the founding meeting of the Constructivist group OSA, with whom Golosov was for a time active until he found their technical concerns and preoccupation with design method increasingly antipathetic. Golosov and Melnikov had forged a close alliance in the first few years of the VKhUTEMAS, as a middle way between the extreme avant-gardists and the traditionalists led by Zholtovsky.[68] Indicating that they, too, had a respect for history, they called their studio The New Academy and declared:

Architectural research should consist of the application of well-mastered principles of study to the best monuments of historical architecture. Composition, as an exercise in the principles which have been mastered through experience and by experimental demonstration, is the achievement of a matching between creative intuition and the task posed.[69]

This emphasis on "creative intuition" as the architect's main design tool was to remain constant for both of them and particularly distinguished them from the Constructivists. Most forcefully, Melnikov later rejected that group's interest in method, declaring, "There is no obligatory sequence whatsoever" that is applicable in the design process, which "very much depends on intuition."[70]

The basis of Melnikov's own approach was the pursuit of a single, relatively simple generating idea for each building through exercise of the "creative imagination." For the Palace of Labor project, for example, it was the principle that "every person in an audience of 8,000 can hear a natural voice"; in the Rusakov Club, the transformability of the auditoriums for different-sized audiences (fig. 22); in the echelon planning of his Sukharev market or the little commercial pavilions in Paris, the idea that "every kiosk has a 'corner site.'"[71] Melnikov detested the teamwork that was fundamental to the Constructivist

Fig. 22. Konstantin Melnikov, trade-union club named for I. V. Rusakov, for workers of the Moscow municipality, 1927–28. Photograph: C. Cooke.

approach. "Creativity," he once said, "is when you can say 'that is mine.'"[72] Ilia Golosov's development of their early ideas combined elements of many other currents. With the Rationalists he believed that form must have "meaning." The basic process of design consisted in transforming "mass," which is semantically inarticulate, into "form, which is responsible to the meaning that has brought it into existence." There were echoes of Zholtovsky in Golosov's insistence that the objective of composition was "harmony," although his harmony was a balancing of the "visual dynamics of the configurations of masses and forms employed, in relation to their repose or dynamism."[73]

Golosov was highly prolific, and as the perspective of his entry for the 1926 Electrobank competition shows (plate 51), he had all the professional control characteristic of the older generation. But some of his formal motifs occur just too often to be genuine originality: the glazed circular corner tower, for example, became almost a trademark. The best-known built demonstration of this motif was his Zuev Club, still standing in central Moscow. Like Melnikov's buildings, it has one key viewpoint that encapsulates an image of the building, but for all their insistence on composition, proportion, and harmony, most other viewpoints are much less satisfactory.

Another important member of the somewhat older generation of the avant-garde was Grigori Barkhin, whose famous *Izvestiia* building of 1926–27 (plate 54) was a job of unusual prestige for its time. *Izvestiia,* as the voice of the Party Central Committee, had its headquarters constructed and detailed to an almost pre-revolutionary standard. Such details as its bronze door fittings are still in superb condition today. The original scheme had a twelve-story central tower that led all his contemporaries to call it a "skyscraper." Like various such projects of this date, it ran afoul of new height limitations imposed by the Moscow City Soviet. Even as finally constructed, the building, with its smooth surfaces and boldly expressed frame, rose above the two- and three-storied Classical vernacular of Moscow as a symbol of the new age that powerfully expressed the dream of urbanism they fostered. A building stylistically similar to Barkhin's that suffered the same height cut was the nearby Gostorg headquarters (fig. 23) by a pre-revolutionary colleague of the Vesnins', Boris Velikovsky, and some of the younger Constructivists. Period photographs of the Gostorg interior convey the transparency and the dynamic movements of circulation which they, like their Western *confrères,* identified as key elements of the modern spatial experience.[74]

A stalwart of MAO, Barkhin was typical of the older professionals in pursuing modernism without theoretical rhetoric. He later wrote:

However theoretical or even at times abstract the problems with which I had to deal, I always believed that one's analysis and one's conclusions must be closely intertwined with live practice, and with the urgent concerns of the present moment. As I see it, this is entirely appropriate to architecture, which is simultaneously the most abstract and the most practical of all the arts.[75]

Given Shchusev's age and background, it is at first perhaps surprising to find him among the modernists. Like many of the older men, he would probably never have labeled himself an avant-gardist. A better term for these designers

Fig. 23. Boris Velikovsky with Mikhail Barshch et al. Headquarters building for Gostorg, Miasnitskaia (Kirov) Street, Moscow, 1925–27, interior view on the main staircase. From *Ezhegodnik MAO* (MAO Annual), no. 6, Moscow, 1930, p. 39.

would be "pragmatic modernist," and pragmatism was indeed central to Shchusev's approach. In a lecture given in 1926, he reflected the inevitable yearning of one who had built "before," under conditions of less exigency:

Style is not a product of the particular tastes of a few people. Style is a system of how things are decorated.... At the present time, we cannot aspire to the luxuriant. We must merely give form to that which derives directly from construction of the simplest forms.

Is this architecture? Does this represent its demise or its flowering? Simple treatments are closer to the latter than the former.... If we proceed from the demands of today, we must take account of the fact that right now, the most expensive materials are brick and glass. All contemporary design, based on the simple forms of concrete, brick and glass, therefore shows itself to be not economic. On the contrary: all these aspirations to produce something economic crumble to dust as a result of the high cost of plate glass.... There is no way we can talk about architecture in today's context.[76]

For a man who spent much time in planning work and official or administrative affairs, Shchusev left a substantial modernist oeuvre and explored a wide range of new building types (plate 58). Perhaps his masterpiece of this decade is the Lenin Mausoleum (plates 55 and 57), which is a superb piece of contextualism as well as exquisite monumentality.

Providing a glimpse of the other end of the building spectrum, mass housing, are two very typical schemes for different Moscow sites (plates 61 and 63) by Mikhail Motylev, a young architect who graduated from the Moscow College in the middle of the war. Such blocks were typical elements of the new residential complexes that became the

Soviet norm by the middle twenties. Kindergartens, basic shopping, and probably some collective laundry facilities were integrated among the minimal apartments.

Typically the open space here would not be treated with the garden-city care for detail that is seen in Gegello's earlier drawing from Leningrad, but such housing represented a dramatic environmental improvement for workers previously living in slum basements. The relatively conventional apartments provided in such structures were heavily criticized by the Constructivists as contributing nothing to a gradual "socialization" of the inhabitants' lifestyle or psychology. Their own design research in housing was aimed at producing complexes that would be more active social catalysts.[77]

Radicalism in the schools

Even as building activity reached a high pitch again in the later twenties, most of the leading architects continued teaching. Whereas student designs of the early twenties were often highly diagrammatic, strongly reflecting the lack of real building around them as well as the inexperience of many of their young teachers, the later twenties saw a flowering of imaginative student work, both in school and for the numerous open competitions. Through these channels many students contributed as much as their elders to the development of Soviet society's new building types, including educational and medical facilities, complexes related to mass feeding such as bread factories, food markets, factory kitchens, and dining halls, as well as industrial buildings and, of course, housing and the planning of new social districts. But none of this hard realism quenched student inventiveness, as shown by two projects, one from a Rationalist, the other from a Constructivist.

Georgi Krutikov was one of Ladovsky's students who assisted him in many investigations in the psychotechnical laboratory. Within that program he conducted his own research project entitled "On the path to a mobile architecture: its social, technical and formal foundations." His work derived from the conviction that "today's dead, immobile and inconvenient planning of our towns must in future be replaced by *mobile planning* based on new principles of spatial solution. It is already our task, as the architect-inventors of today, to assist in the birth of such a mobile architecture."[78]

His final diploma project, presented in 1928, comprised two parts: sixteen explanatory panels with collaged images analyzing the problem, and his own proposals for the city of the future based on flying (plates 79–85).

Nikolai Sokolov had spent time in Ladovsky's laboratory, too, but his project of the same year (plates 86–88) was done in Vesnin's studio and published immediately in their journal, *Contemporary Architecture*. Criticized by some as a type of "workers' leisure hotel" that dangerously fostered individualism,[79] his little cylindrical pods in their arcadian greenery present a dream almost as unattainable in the Soviet Union then as Krutikov's, and are also accompanied by a lively argument of collaged images.

Both projects were too obviously fanciful to have a serious influence. One of the most outstandingly original of the previous year's diploma projects in Vesnin's studio, however—for a Lenin Institute of Librarianship by the young

OSA member Ivan Leonidov (fig. 24)[80]—had already become something of a liability to the public reputation, even credibility, of the Constructivist architects. They were by now a very serious and practice-oriented group, with important state-sponsored work on new housing types, for example, well under way. Suddenly their students were being distracted from reality for a world of high technology and platonic volumes. Ginzburg quickly issued a *rappel à l'ordre* in their journal. Leonidov's drawings and model were marvelous, he agreed, offering valuable new thinking in a "space-oriented architectural treatment which leads away from the traditional conception of building, towards a reorganization of the very

concept of the public space and the city in which such a building might stand." His means were boldly Constructive, "technically feasible and theoretically applicable." However, he went on, "Leonidov at the same time creates something *which it is economically impossible to realize today.* Having taken a bold leap out of ordinariness, he has fallen into a certain *utopianism.* That utopianism consists not only in the fact that the USSR is not now economically strong enough to erect such building, but also in the fact that *Leonidov was not really able to prove that his constructive conundrum was actually necessary, i.e., that this solution and only this will solve the problem concerned.*" His work was "a landmark for our future work," but "we must still not forget about the real conditions in which our practical activities have to take place."[81]

The sort of site planning and urban spaces that were developing in mainstream modernist work, characterized by the "free asymmetries" of functional composition of which Ginzburg had spoken earlier, are exemplified by such large building projects of this period as the new Lenin State Library for central Moscow, the Soviet equivalent of the Library of Congress. The Vesnin brothers' project had won the first stage of the competition, and their designs went through several variants.[82] All were characterized by the same functional planning and free massing, with extensive use of courtyards within the site (plates 65 and 66). Typically more concerned with dramatic and monolithic massing is the project by a group under Vladimir Fidman, an ASNOVA founder member and contemporary of Ladovsky.

What we are in fact seeing in Leonidov's work is the introduction of the Suprematist formal system into Constructivism, though neither Leonidov nor Ginzburg spoke in those terms. It is also, I would contend, a rural Russian sensibility, owing much not just to Leonidov's peasant origins but also to

Fig. 24. Ivan Leonidov, VKhUTEMAS diploma project for a Lenin Institute of Librarianship, 1927: photograph of the model. Courtesy A. Kopp.

his ascetic philosophy and personal be-
lief in a certain purposeful discomfort,
even mortification of the flesh, as part
of the tempering of "a true man."[83] A
typically peasant philosophy, it is the
very opposite of that pursuit of convenience and time-saving derived from
Western urbanism, and from the
industrial-planning models of Taylorism
and Henry Ford, which inspired Constructivist work.[84] The different design
approaches of Leonidov and orthodox
Constructivism are most clearly contrasted where they tackled a common
brief. In this exhibition, projects by the
Vesnin brothers and Leonidov for the
cultural complex of Moscow's Proletarsky district provide just such a
comparison. The building type was an
enlarged version of the workers' club.
The site was the historic former
Simonov Monastery, and there were projects in the competition, such as that by
Zholtovsky's pupil Golts, which fully
restored and converted the historic
buildings of the monastery.

In a project of 1928 Leonidov called The
Club of New Social Type (plates 72–75),
his spatial thinking moved to truly
Suprematist scale in systems of "spatial
organization of cultural services,"
extending far beyond the distribution of
volumes on a typical club site.[85] His Palace of Culture competition entry of 1930
treated the site itself as a line of four
square territories, each organized by a
planning grid of 4 by 4 squares. The
physical-education center (plates 76 and
77) was one of these territories, others
being designated for open-air public
meetings and festivals, a great multi-
purpose circular "theater" for mass
assemblies, political meetings, and
performances, and a "scientific and
historical sector" with libraries and
resource centers. Far from being just a
local facility, his project would create "a
methodological center with cells all over
the USSR ... linked to all other possible
institutions." Other functions specified
in the brief, such as public canteens,
kindergartens, and normal educational
accommodation were dispersed throughout the Proletarsky district itself.[86]

Even Georgi Krutikov, known for his
fantasist designs, felt compelled to com-
ment in the architectural press that
"the project had to be rejected because
there is no realistic basis at present for
implementing a cultural combine on
this model."[87] More orthodox critics like
Leonidov's exact contemporary in the
VKhUTEMAS, Alexander Karra, attacked
the buildings as "barracks," the spaces
as "deserts." He abhorred the project's
complete abstractness and dismissed its
claims to "functional organization" as
merely "a verbal raincoat." "The workers
consistently demand a high emotional
content in buildings," he insisted. "They
require the materialized expression of
the power of their class."[88]

This was the opinion of a rising young
leader of the new "proletarian" architects' organization, VOPRA, formed in
1929, who were struggling for professional ascendency over the by now
"establishment" avant-garde. We see here
the battle lines emerging between the
conflicting views of "proletarian" architectural language that Lunacharsky's
pronouncements had made inevitable.
Leonidov was the Constructivists'
Achilles heel. As VOPRA liked to put it,
"Leonidovism ... embodies all that is
most negative in constructivism and
formalism" (by which they meant Rationalism).[89] VOPRA was the assertion
of another kind of pragmatic modernism, with non-Russian cultural roots,
whose strongholds were in the
republican centers of Armenia, the
Ukraine, Georgia, Tomsk in Siberia, and
to some extent Leningrad. Its adherents
were architects who saw no reason to
be dictated to by old-style Russian gen-
tlemen of what they considered dubious
class origins like the Vesnins and
Ginzburg.[90]

As it was designed and built over the next few years by the Vesnins, the Palace of Culture for the Proletarsky district of Moscow was everything that the project of their pupil Leonidov had failed to be. As the perspectives of the final building show (plates 67 and 68), it was a classic piece of tight modernist planning, pleasantly scaling the surrounding open spaces and answering the brief as set. Like much of the Vesnins' work, it lacked the refined proportions and that extra rigor which Ginzburg would have given it (sadly none of his work from this period is in the Shchusev Museum's collection). But it is not impossible to imagine it as a better bit of VOPRA work from this date.

Even more of a loner than Leonidov, working entirely outside the main professional framework of the avant-garde, was another highly inventive synthesizer of Suprematism with the formal language of Constructivism, Iakov Chernikhov. He had trained at the Imperial St. Petersburg Academy, but the rigorous program in "spatial construction" which he devised was taught by him mainly to youngsters in Leningrad technical schools rather than to incipient architects. In a series of books he expounded his theory of how architectural form should be generated according to the basic principles of volumetric assembly demonstrated in the construction of machines. The books did not emerge until after 1930, but Chernikhov's work had been seen in exhibitions he staged in the late twenties. His vignettes of industrial architecture, like his superb imaginative compositions of "constructive buildings" of the future, represented a technical sophistication that was then unattainable in the Soviet Union but gave explicit form to a world that remained implicit in so much avant-garde imagery and thinking.[91]

The six years occupied by the final design and building of the Vesnins' Palace of Culture complex saw the climax of the stylistic confrontation that had been brewing throughout the twenties. Its final denouement took place through two major competitions for prestigious state buildings on sites of symbolic centrality in Moscow, adjacent to the Kremlin. The first, and most protracted, from 1931 to 1934, was for a so-called Palace of Soviets to stand beside the river just west of the Kremlin (fig. 25). The second, a simpler affair in 1934, was for the headquarters of the government ministry most important to the Soviet Union's whole economic effort, the Commissariat of Heavy Industry, called Narkomtiazhprom.

Denouement: the Palace of Soviets competition

In both physical size and ideological burden, the Palace of Soviets was an enlarged version of the Palace of Labor of 1923.[92] Such was the scale of the conception that the new Palace was to contain halls for six thousand and fifteen thousand people, as well as numerous smaller auditoriums. When the brief was issued in July 1931, it said nothing explicit about style. The only aesthetic requirements were that it should be "monumental" and "fit in artistically with the general architectural scheme of Moscow."[93]

Design research had actually started at the beginning of that year when a dozen architects and teams were invited to prepare preliminary proposals that would assist in clarifying the options and priorities. The invitation list was heavily weighted in favor of the modernists, including ASNOVA, its recent splinter group ARU, Ladovsky, the Constructivists now renamed SASS, and the Leningrad Constructivist leader Alexander Nikolsky. From the engineering-oriented old guard were Genrich Liudvig

Fig. 25. Moscow River, looking past the Kremlin walls, right, toward the Cathedral of Christ the Savior, by Konstantin Ton, designed in 1832 as a pantheon to the victory over Napoleon. The cathedral was demolished to build the Palace of Soviets: postcard ca. 1905.

and German Krasin. There were only three representatives of the more historicist persuasions: Shchusev and the brothers Boris and Dmitri Iofan, the former lately returned from many years in Rome.[94]

These design teams worked from February to May 1931. In June the focus was sharpened when Moscow Party Secretary Lazar Kaganovich delivered a major policy speech to a plenum of the Party Central Committee, which laid down policy in town planning and the development of public utilities in Soviet towns. At last, under the government's second Five Year Plan for economic development, the basic repair and modernization of the inherited urban fabrics were to be started, as well as the major expansion of new industrial centers. In calling for "serious Marxist-theoretical bases for our practice in these areas," Kaganovich deplored the lack of any parallel theoretical base in the field of architecture. Architects, he said, "must devise an architectural formulation of the [Soviet] town that will give it the necessary beauty."[95] This became the agenda for a competition that was one of the great turning points in Soviet architectural history.

The preliminary schemes were exhibited and published in July/August 1931. With an international open competition announced for the Palace, these schemes received official criticism from a special committee under Lunacharsky, which revealed the direction being taken by government thinking.

Accurately enough, the committee declared: "The preliminary projects reflect the battle of ideological directions in Soviet architecture, beginning with the rightward aspirations to preserve the golden cupolas of the cathedral of Christ Savior [which awaited demolition on site], and ending with the ultra-leftist exercises of ASNOVA and the super-industrialistic proposals of ARU and others."[96]

Much of the criticism at this stage was functional and well justified. Thus Ladovsky was faulted because he "says not a word about how he will tackle the acoustic problems inherent to his hemispherical auditorium" (plates 102 and 103), and "he considers superfluous the factor specially stressed in the brief that the site must have space for parades."[97] One ARU drawing (plate 97) shows a scheme with parades in progress, but the committee pointed out that "their main auditorium is totally unresolved and its fully glazed vertical sides will make it an unusable hothouse." On the aesthetic side, this scheme "seems to think a monument to the first Five Year Plan has to look like a factory, with hangars, chimneys, etc., even though they have no functional relevance here."[98]

Shchusev was seen as having produced "a realistic project," but here, too, "simplicity of aesthetic treatment gives the building an industrial character inappropriate to the Palace of Soviets."[99] Boris Iofan had distributed the accommodation at two ends of an open classical courtyard: this attracted criticism because it was "too spread out and looks more like a conglomeration of unrelated elements than a Palace of Soviets." Some specific, if rather incoherent, aesthetic prejudices were clearly beginning to manifest themselves. Ironically, in relation to the project with which he would finally win, Iofan's "placing on his central

tower of a vast figure of a worker, imitating the American Statue of Liberty, gives the project a pseudo-proletarian character."[100]

Among those accused of being "super-industrialistic" were certainly the pair representing the Constructivist group, SASS: Mikhail Kuznetsov and Leonid Pavlov, who was a close friend of Leonidov. Leonidov was probably out of town, as he spent most of 1931 on planning work in the provinces. But whether or not the scheme secretly bears his hand, it is formally and conceptually a direct successor to his Palace of Culture. The drawings in the exhibition (plates 94 and 95) show the building itself, which is placed on one corner of the site. They indicate why the committee wrote, "The building's whole construction of steel and glass with deliberately stressed use of unnecessary technical elements constitutes a model of technological fetishism." This made it an example of "the bourgeois trend in architecture, which is ideologically alien to proletarian architecture." But there was worse: what these drawings of the building do not show is that "the only accommodation placed on the site is the large auditorium. Everything else is distributed in a great circle across the map of Moscow.... This is done in order to provide an open sports field near the main hall, where "mass assemblies" and physical culture routines can be performed in the open air."[101]

In generalizing the lessons of this preliminary, closed stage of the competition, the committee addressed the question of how the balance of functionality and symbolism in this building should compare with what was "normally" appropriate. It was decided that the principle of "form being determined by the functions of internal accommodation" was a "necessary, but not sufficient principle" in this case because "the Palace of Soviets must also be a monumental building, an outstanding artistic and architectural monument of the Soviet capital, characterizing the epoch and embodying the urge of the workers towards the building of communism."[102]

The committee's critiques of individual projects reveal how certain formal characteristics already had symbolic loading in their emerging lexicon. Almost everyone had "forgotten about proportions," the committee said, and about "scaling their monolithic volumes to the human being." Familiar at least with Constructivist jargon, they also provided a first positive recipe for the means by which the "embodiment" of values might be achieved.

The functional method of design must be supplemented by a corrective: an artistic treatment of the form. All the spatial arts must be employed here: architecture (which gives proportionality of the parts), painting (which uses color), sculpture (for richness of light and dark), in combination with lighting technology and the art of the theatrical producer.[103]

The international open competition proceeded under these guidelines. The foreign entrants probably did not know how the dice had already been loaded. Barkhin described them as "in general, very disappointing,"[104] but among the several American entrants was one fine piece of modernistic monumentality by Hector Hamilton. When Hamilton got a prize but Le Corbusier's superb project was dismissed (fig. 26), the direction of the jury's taste was beginning to be clear. Most of the foreign entries were more or less ignored, but Corbusier's was singled out for particular criticism as "cultivating the aesthetic of a complicated machine that is to 'turn over' huge masses of humanity."[105]

Hamilton shared the three-way first prize with Zholtovsky and a redesigned scheme by Boris Iofan. One Zholtovsky perspective appears in this exhibition (plate 107), besides the project of young VOPRA member Alexander Karra (plates 99 and 100). Also included is one of the numerous pseudonymous popular entries (plate 98), which unites the two vast auditoriums into one "fully serviced version of Red Square."

In March 1932 thirteen designers were asked to develop their projects further by July of that year; on his own initiative Hamilton went to Moscow to rework his scheme (fig. 27). In the middle of this period, on April 23, the Party Central Committee issued a decision "On

Fig. 26. Le Corbusier, model for the Palace of Soviets competition, 1931. The Museum of Modern Art, New York. Purchase.

Reformation of Literary and Artistic Organizations," which sounded the death knell for architectural associations with independent design philosophies.[106] On July 18, with the formation of a single Union of Soviet Architects, all such associations were abolished. The new Union's board contained a catholic representation of viewpoints,[107] but the years of diversity, when architects could pursue an appropriate aesthetic independent of political pressure, were over. Meanwhile, the Party Central Committee decreed that the future of Soviet architecture, as of the other arts and culture, lay in Socialist Realism.

Socialist Realism in architecture was always defined as "not a style but a

method," and its key principle, as in other fields, was "critical assimilation of the heritage."[108] By this was meant the identification and carrying forward of those elements of the traditional culture or aesthetic system that still had positive ideological associations, and building a new synthesis of these with the latest technological possibilities. *Izvestiia* warned that "assimilation does not mean copying the past: it is a creative activity of upward march from the peaks of former culture towards new achievements."[109] Certain indications of how this might be achieved were provided in competition-jury commentaries, but "critical assimilation" was hard to demonstrate with positive examples. Hence they focused on identifying non-"critical" modes of borrowing and reminders that "architecture, as an active art," must utilize the full potential of painting and sculpture to augment its message.[110]

That summer the new Palace of Soviets variants were pronounced "somewhat better."[111] Iofan had drawn everything into one dumpy stepped tower and removed the offending statue.[112] Ginzburg's scheme represents this stage (plate 101). Not surprisingly, he was not among the five groups asked to continue further,[113] but the Vesnin brothers were. Their handsome perspective for this next stage (plates 104 and 105) was executed for them by the Stenberg brothers, former pioneers of Constructivism in the early days of Inkhuk and subsequently established graphic designers. The experienced Leningrad partnership of Shchuko and Vladimir Gelfreikh produced an uncharacteristically literal piece of Italianism (plate 106). Iofan's scheme at this stage was still a dumpy wedding cake of three circular drums, each one cased in a continuous classical colonnade. Its stepped profile was very characteristically Russian: the towers of the Kremlin walls alongside offered the geographically

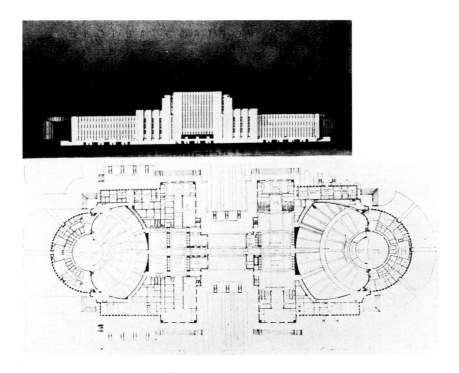

Fig. 27.   Hector Hamilton, entry for the second (open) stage of the Palace of Soviets competition, Moscow, 1931: main elevation to Moscow River. From *Architectural Review* (London), May 1932, p. 200.

closest example of a well-understood formal prototype. The Sukharev tower, then still standing farther north in the city, was an even more famous example. The lower levels of Iofan's design were now more expansively extended than in his previous version to make a forecourt and mass parade ground. On the front edge of the topmost drum stood an athletic little figure, some eighteen meters high, representing "liberated labor." The overall height of the building was 250 meters.[114]

In the Construction Committee's judgment on this stage, Iofan's latest version was "taken as the basis for a final design," but in its announcement the committee decreed that "the upper part of the Palace of Soviets should be topped by a powerful sculpture of Lenin, 50 to 75 meters high, so that the Palace of Soviets should have the appearance of being a pedestal for the figure of Lenin." Further clauses "instructed comrade Iofan to continue working on the design in this direction" and indicated that other architects might be brought in to join him.[115]

From its relatively rough finish, the drawing by Iofan and his assistants (plate 108) seems to have been an early response to this demand for incorporation of a vast sculpture of Lenin. (There is apparently no exact dating for it.) A measure of the seriousness with which this whole scheme was now treated officially, and the cultural scope that architecture had now acquired, is given by the composition of a Standing Architectural and Technical Committee set up three weeks after the decision, on June 4, 1932. Among the thirty-two names, the architects were Iofan himself, Shchuko and Gelfreikh (now appointed as his collaborators), Shchusev, Zholtovsky, Viktor Vesnin, Genrich Liudvig, Arkady Mordvinov, and thirty-five-year-old president of the new Union of

Architects Karo Alabian as secretary. On the technical side were structural engineers German Krasin and Artur Loleit, also Nikolai Shvernik, ex-head of the Metalworkers Union and now chairman of the Central Union of Trade Unions; Pavel Rottert, newly appointed chief engineer of the metro construction project, and chief city planner of Moscow Vladimir Semionov. They were joined by painters Isaac Brodsky, Kuzma Petrov-Vodkin, Ilia Mashkov, and Fedor Fedorovsky; by monumental sculptors Matvei Maniser, Sergei Merkurov, and Ivan Shadr; by theater directors Vsevolod Meyerhold and Konstantin Stanislavsky; by the art critic and historian from the pre-revolutionary *World of Art* circle Igor Grabar; by the writer, now chief theorist of Socialist Realism in literature, Maxim Gorky. Representing the political establishment, Lunacharsky was joined by Gleb Krzhizhanovsky, a Bolshevik of impeccable credentials since before the 1905 revolution, leader of major projects like the GOELRO plan for electrifying Russia in the early twenties, and then chairman of the State Planning Bureau Gosplan, now president of the Academy of Sciences and Deputy Commissar for Enlightenment for the Russian Republic.[116]

What role these people played is less clear than the nature of the architectural task such a committee defined. The final scheme was a more refined version of the Iofan scheme shown here, with Lenin enlarged to "the height of a twenty-five story skyscraper" so that his index finger alone was a twenty-foot cantilever. With an overall height of 415 meters, it was now "the tallest and volumetrically largest building in the world".[117] Working drawings "sufficient for a start on construction" were to be ready by May 1, 1934,[118] but even with that Standing Committee at their elbow, December 1934 saw Iofan, Shchuko, Gelfreikh, and others setting off for Europe and the United States, touring New York, Washington, and Chicago to absorb the necessary technical expertise.[119] Meanwhile, another major architectural competition was under way just the other side of the Kremlin, offering the first opportunity for exploration of the new aesthetic guidelines.

Assimilation of the heritage

If the Palace of Soviets was the focus and symbol of the new social and political order, the Commissariat of Heavy Industry performed similar roles for the industrial policy on which that order was being built. The site ran along one whole side of Red Square in the area that had been Russia's commercial and trading center in pre-revolutionary times.[120] The invited competition entrants were the big names of the twenties: ex-Constructivists Ginzburg, the Vesnins, and Leonidov; ex-Rationalists Fidman and Fridman; independents Panteleimon Golosov and Melnikov; Classicist Fomin and four teams of relatively unknown worthies.[121] Competitors could demolish structures around the site, and some proposed to remove St. Basil's as well as most of the old business district. On the other hand, as the new official architecture journal put it, "Unlike in most sites of reconstruction ... the architect is forced here to be concerned with elements of our architectural heritage that are of absolutely exceptional importance both aesthetically and historically."[122]

To handle that context in accordance with principles of "critical assimilation of the heritage" was no small challenge. Most of the entrants produced large, sometimes hideously monolithic vol-

umes in an eclectic mode, which stood as static implants amid the extraordinary richness of the historic environment. Three versions of the Vesnins' scheme (plates 109–11) show them playing variations on a theme, all harking back to the images of high-rise modernist urbanism that they had discussed enthusiastically in the very first issue of their journal in 1926 after seeing Hugh Ferriss's drawings and Erich Mendelsohn's book of photographs, *Amerika*.[123] Two designs by the younger stars of the former avant-garde, however, rose to an entirely different level of inventiveness. The schemes of Melnikov and Leonidov offer a fascinating contrast in their response to the demands for monumentality and rhetoric. If the avant-garde had a final fling to show the extraordinary breadth of its architectural talents, it was here.

Melnikov's scheme (plates 112 and 113) is almost a pathology of the principle that one single idea shall generate a design. The plan was generated by two Vs, or Roman numeral fives, as Melnikov states, "to strengthen in this building the emotional expression of having achieved the objectives of the first Five Year Plan."[124] His synthesis of contemporaneity and the architectural heritage rested on an obvious and easily read symbolism combined with the bold use of what, for the USSR, were relatively advanced technologies of iron- and concrete-framed construction and giant open-air escalators (plates 114 and 115). There were forty-one stories above ground. What the drawings do not show clearly is that the Red Square side is deeply excavated to light sixteen floors below ground level.[125] The result was a richly three-dimensional dissolution of the ground surface into the building volume in the tradition of Futurist visions of the modern city. But Red Square is

dominated by the great axial symmetry of the two wings "linked together by common external mechanized stairs to manifest the rapidly rising line of reconstruction in our heavy industry today."[126]

On a domestic scale, symmetry was characteristic of classical Moscow, certainly, but on this gargantuan scale it was totally alien to the balance of architectural monuments Melnikov had so carefully preserved. His words indicate that he did seek to make some scalar integration:

By the arcading under the staircases the whole forty-storied height of the building is gradually reduced to the horizontal plane of Red Square, and by the same token its architectural scale is preserved, with the remarkable Kremlin cathedrals, the Lenin mausoleum and St. Basil's.[127]

Competitors could choose to retain or demolish St. Basil's Cathedral. Interestingly, it was the leading avant-gardists who kept it, whereas Fomin, Panteleimon Golosov, Fridman, and the lesser figures seemed unable to cope with its proximity and proposed its demolition.

Melnikov's sculptural imagery combined heroic figures with circular propylaea like slices cut from the bearings of some great drive shaft. It creates extraordinary ocular vignettes, as his compelling perspective of one entrance shows (plate 116). Lissitzky attacked the scheme as "so loaded up with tastelessness and provincialism that I am embarrassed for him."[128] Viktor Balikhin, who ten years earlier as a fellow member in ASNOVA had been much concerned with the art-architecture relationship, wrote viciously of Melnikov's symbolism here: "All this monumental window dressing is shot through with old-fashioned and primitive forms of modernistic symbolism."[129] Though more refined in its draftsmanship, it does indeed recall most strongly the romantic symbolism of the early post-revolutionary years. Fomin's Paris pavilion project is the closest example to that in this exhibition. (Fomin himself had interestingly almost eliminated art elements from his design for Narkomtiazhprom.) But the difference of mood since 1924 perfectly reflected the course which the intervening ten years had run. Fomin's cheerful muscularity is gone. Here in Melnikov's Narkomtiazhprom the medium is hyperbole. The mood is deeply menacing, deeply ironic, and deeply reflects the political conjuncture of the moment.

Leonidov's project, by contrast, made its historical references to pre-Classical traditions of medieval Russia. In a purely architectural sense, this far better reflected the surrounding context of the site. In the now approved sense of "use of the other arts," he did not conform. In terms of "critical assimilation of the heritage," however, his project was masterly, uncompromisingly modern in its construction yet referring subtly to immediate and deeper historical contexts.

Here, all activities specified in the brief are located on the site. With the strong feeling for the tensions between volumes in space that is pure Suprematism, the separate elements of Leonidov's building, and the complex as a whole, set up a new set of energetic relationships across this symbolically rich but confused city center. By this means, he weaves a new and self-consistent composition into the hitherto rather disordered urban fabric, thereby enlarging its scale from the medieval to the twenty-first century, whereas Melnikov and the rest had cre-

ated a dramatic rupture. Melnikov's powerful axiality had been very awkward, and his "dip downward" competed unhappily for attention with the existing descent of Red Square to the river on the other axis. Leonidov's scheme, by contrast, makes a naturally scaled and purposeful seam with the surrounding city in each of its four directions: completing Red Square with a tribune for parades, completing the Classical square to the north, and addressing the Bolshoi Theater with the subtle polychrome paraboloid over the workers' club, which simultaneously addresses St. Basil's to the south.[130] The stroke of genius, however, is the group of three towers of differing form, whose relationship to Moscow's former great vertical, the Ivan bell tower of the Kremlin, is indicated in a montage and a small sketch (plate 120).[131]

Those images give an objective description of the formal composition but do not indicate the deeper reference they make to traditional Russian typologies. Herein, of course, lies the "critical assimilation," but the motif that has been "critically" reused is not at the level of surface decoration or style. It is a compositional motif that has profound roots in Russian traditional architecture. A cluster of three geometrically dissimilar tower forms was the traditional form of the *pogost,* which constituted the spiritual and commercial heart of the old Russian village. The most famous remaining *pogost* is at Kizhi in North Russia (fig. 28). In his Narkomtiazhprom project, we see Leonidov drawing a symbolic parallel between the organizational type deeply embedded in Russian history and culture and the Commissariat of Heavy Industry of the

Soviet era, which is entirely apposite. To the Soviet state of the early thirties, this Commissariat was the organization that propagated and enacted the Soviet government's dogma of political progress through a development led by heavy industry, and the parallel he implies between that dogma and the dogma of the Orthodox Church was an accurate one, indeed not in essence novel.

The focal role of the *pogost* as symbol and locational node in the landscape was established by its asymmetry, which is again the key factor in Leonidov's composition. From every direction the profile was different, as the three different tower elements separate and coalesce according to the viewer's

Fig. 28. Kizhi *pogost,* North Russia, view with the three vertical elements clustered together. From Igor Grabar, *Istoriia russkago iskusstva: istoriia arkhitektury, tom.1, do-petrovskaia epokha* (History of Russian art: history of architecture, vol. 1: pre-Petrine period), Moscow, 1910, p. 442.

movement across the landscape. Using that dynamic device, Leonidov's design offers a new focal point for central Moscow. As his montage showed, the building was intended as a compositional replacement for the Ivan bell tower of the Kremlin, whose single vertical was historically the city's symbolic and visual focus. But the other paradigm, of the *pogost,* had split the Ivan bell tower form into three parts while giving the image twentieth-century scale.

That dynamism and multi-directionality were in sharp contrast to the static monolith of the Palace of Soviets, then under construction (though never finished), as the focal pair at the heart of socialism. Each of Leonidov's three towers has an origin in the established vocabulary of Russian architecture. The convex, circular tower refers to the rostral columns at the heart of St. Petersburg's commercial center, which are known to all Russians. The square tower represents uncompromising modernity, but with the vertical articulation and crowning profile that create a perfectly composed three-dimensional entity, and the concave tower offers a female complement to the prismatic male forms. The polychrome drum over the workers' club, at the northern end of the podium, addresses the historical paradigm of the richly colored Russian church, of which St. Basil's was the most exotic example in the whole country.

Leonidov's perspective drawing with the Bolshoi Theater in the background (plate 119) is surely one of the most subtle and satisfactory images of all Russian avant-gardism, totally buildable yet richly poetic. As Andrei Gozak has shown, his sketch of a view through the cupolas of St. Basil's (plate 120) and the soaring, upward view with an airplane (plate 124) are actually insertions of his tower into photographs by Erich

Mendelsohn from his *Amerika* and *Russland, Europa und Amerika;* both books were in Leonidov's library.[132] They provide an apposite final symbol of the cross-cultural debt running through the whole decade.

Leonidov's Narkomtiazhprom offers a subtle demonstration of how the modernist language can be enriched through genuinely "critical assimilation" of formal aspects of an aesthetic heritage, how a synthesis may be produced that owes nothing to applied decorative emblems. In my judgment it is perhaps the finest example from any Soviet architect of what "the method of Socialist Realism" could achieve in skilled hands.[133] Needless to say, that is not how it was seen at the time. Lissitzky managed to credit Leonidov with being "the only competitor who, as is evident from his series of drawings, tried to find a unity for the new complex formed by the Kremlin, St. Basil's Cathedral and the new building." However, he dismissed it on the grounds that "in practical terms, he gets no further than a kind of stage set."[134]

Elsewhere in the official architectural press, the schemes of Leonidov and Melnikov were grouped together, despite their being actually so different, "reminding us of that period in the development of Soviet architecture when such utopianism was considered a form of compulsory virtue, and when the creation of architectural abstractions was considered to display 'progressive' architectural thinking." Today, however, continued this editorial in the official journal of the Union of Architects in late 1934, "they look like an accidental anachronism" and "make us feel vexed disappointment toward the authors who have misused their talents for artistic and spatial invention."[135]

Unlike the Palace of Soviets contest, Narkomtiazhprom never produced a winner, far less a start on site. For that we must be thankful: like the Palace, it could never have been completed in the USSR at that date. Today the unfinished foundations of the Palace of Soviets are an open-air swimming pool, and the nineteenth-century Cathedral of Christ the Savior was no great loss. On the other hand, replacement of the GUM department-store galleria by some crude, half-finished foundations would have been a disaster amid the rich historical ensemble of Red Square.

The Palace venture was the medium through which the central issue of the proper social and aesthetic basis for Soviet architecture was resolved, and Narkomtiazhprom reinforced it. After ten years of consistent statements by Lunacharsky, the outcome cannot really have been a surprise. As I have described here, technological limitations made some of the decisions unavoidable; the Party had made the other decisions inevitable early in the twenties. But the two were inseparable; the Soviet Union was not an advanced country akin to the West. The first buildings of the avant-garde, in the middle twenties, were addressed to the small pockets of urban working class—relatively sophisticated and habituated to objects with a technological aesthetic—who had a glimmer of understanding at least of such concepts as rationality and efficiency. By the end of the decade, political and cultural emphasis had shifted, however. A leadership itself mainly of peasant origins was attempting to address the issue of development to the ninety percent of the population who, by any Western standard, were totally nonurbanized. Given these circumstances, it can be no surprise that the aesthetic which prevailed was based on an appeal to popular aesthetic values. Even in the more sophisticated and technically advanced West, the battle has ultimately been much the same.

Notes

1 I. B. Shub, "Stroitel'stvo v gody vosstanovitel'skogo protsessa 1923/4–1926/7" (Construction in the years of the restoration process, 1923/4–1926/7), *Planovoe khoziastvo* (The Planned Economy) (Moscow), 1926, no. 10, pp. 43–56.

2 A range of these new types and a comparison with their post-revolutionary equivalents may be found in C. Cooke, "Moscow Map Guide 1900–1930," *Architectural Design* (London), 1983, no. 5/6, pp. 81–96.

3 C. Cooke, "Fedor Osipovich Shekhtel: an architect and his clients in turn-of-the-century Moscow," *Architectural Association Files* (London) no. 5, January 1984, pp. 3–31.

4 "Seriia neboskrebov dlia Moskvy: proekt El' Lisitskogo" (A series of skyscrapers for Moscow: project by El Lissitzky), *Izvestiia ASNOVA* (ASNOVA News) (Moscow) no. 1, 1926, pp. 2–3.

5 Page of slogans, *Sovremennaia arkhitektura* (Contemporary Architecture), 1926, no. 3, p. 82.

6 I. Leonidov, "Palitra arkhitektora" (The palette of the architect), *Arkhitektura SSSR* (Architecture USSR) (Moscow) 1934, no. 4, pp. 32–33; for translation and general discussion, see A.Gozak and A. Leonidov, *Ivan Leonidov: The Complete Works* (New York: Rizzoli, 1988).

7 John E. Bowlt, *The Silver Age: Russian Art of the Early Twentieth Century and the World of Art Group* (Newtonville, Mass: Oriental Research Partners, 1982), chapter 2, "Abramtsevo and Talashkino," pp. 28–46; also William Brumfield, "The decorative arts in Russian architecture 1900–1907," *Journal of Decorative and Propaganda Arts* (Miami) no. 5, summer 1987, pp. 12–27.

8 Bowlt, *The Silver Age,* chapters 3–7, on "The World of Art," pp. 47–132.

9 Cooke, "Fedor Osipovich Shekhtel."

10 V. E. Tatlin, "K organizatsii 'khudozhestvnogo obshchestva' na novykh nachalakh" (On the organization of an "artistic society" on new principles), *Nov'* (Virgin Soil), 23 December 1914, p. 10, and "Letter to Benois," 1913; translations in L. A. Zhadova, ed., *Tatlin* (London: Thames & Hudson, 1988), pp. 182–84.

11 For Tatlin, see Zhadova, ed., *Tatlin,* in particular A. A. Strigalev, "From painting to the construction of matter," pp. 13–43; for Malevich, see C. Cooke, "Malevich: from theory into teaching," in *Malevich,* Art and Design Profile no. 15 (New York: St. Martin's Press, 1989), pp. 6–27; and L. Dalrymple Henderson, *The Fourth Dimension and Non-Euclidean Geometry in Modern Art* (Princeton, N.J.: Princeton University Press, 1983), chapter 5.

12 V. E. Tatlin, 'Nasha predstoiashchaia rabota" (The work ahead of us), *VIII S'ezd sovetov: ezhednevnyi buleten* (VIII Congress of Soviets: daily bulletin), 1 January 1921, p. 11. English translations have appeared in Zhadova, ed., *Tatlin,* p. 239, and T. Andersen, *Vladimir Tatlin,* (Stockholm: Moderna Museet, 1968), p. 51, but neither is very exact and in retranslating I have tried to clarify.

13 As in note 12.

14 For discussions, see L. A. Zhadova, "Tatlin: the organizer of material into objects," in Zhadova, ed., *Tatlin,* pp. 134–54; S. O. Khan-Magomedov, *Rodchenko* (London: Thames & Hudson, 1986). Also translated texts in Stephen Bann, ed., *The Tradition of Constructivism* (New York: Viking Press, 1974), section 1, and in John E. Bowlt, ed., *Russian Art of the Avant-Garde: Theory and Criticism 1902–34* (New York: Viking Press, 1976); repub. London: Thames & Hudson, 1989, sections IV and V.

15 For a lively discussion and bibliography, see Alan C. Birnholtz, "El Lissitzky and the spectator: from passivity to participation," in S. Barron and M. Tuchman, eds., *The Avant-Garde in Russia 1910–1930: New Perspectives* (Cambridge, Mass.: MIT Press, 1980), pp. 98–101.

16 Khan-Magomedov, *Rodchenko.*

17 Kandinsky left Russia for the Bauhaus in Germany in 1921 after his concerns for the continued validity of "fine art" became overpowered by the new design-oriented Constructivist lobby in Inkhuk. Gabo felt similarly alienated from current trends and left 'for Berlin in 1922.

18 V. Tolstoy, I. Bibikova, and C. Cooke, eds., *Street Art of the Revolution: Festivals and Celebrations in Russia 1919–33* (London: Thames & Hudson, 1990).

19 J.-L. Cohen, *Le Corbusier et la Mystique de l'URSS* (Paris: Mardaga, 1987), "L'epopée du Centrosojuz," pp. 86–137.

20 For illustration, see Stephen White, *The Bolshevik Poster* (New Haven, Conn.: Yale University Press, 1988), p. 40.

21 Sheila Fitzpatrick, *The Commissariat of Enlightenment: Soviet Organization of Education and the Arts under Lunacharsky* (Cambridge: Cambridge University Press, 1970), chapter 6.

22 Letter of 19 June 1919, quoted from Russian sources in M. I. Astafeva-Dlugach and Iu. p. Volchok, "I Zholtovsky," *Zodchie Moskvy: 2* (Architects of Moscow, vol. 2) (Moscow: Moskovskii rabochii [The Moscow Worker], 1988), pp. 51–52.

23 Some discussion of this appears in S. Frederick Starr, *Melnikov: Solo Architect in a Mass Society* (Princeton, N.J.: Princeton University Press, 1978), pp. 40–41. A group photograph of most members of the Moscow studio appears in S. O. Khan-Magomedov, *Pioneers of Soviet Architecture* (London: Thames & Hudson, 1987), p. 565.

24 Khan-Magomedov, *Pioneers,* p. 67.

25 Numerous other projects on this theme are illustrated in ibid., plates 180–208.

26 Khan-Magomedov, *Rodchenko,* chapter 3; N. Adaskina and D. Sarabianov, *Lioubov Popova* (Paris, 1989).

27 For a detailed discussion including extensive archival documents in translation, see Khan-Magomedov, *Rodchenko,* chapter 4, in particular pp. 83–99. For the visual material, see A. Zander Rudenstein, ed., *Russian Avant-Garde Art: The George Costakis Collection* (London: Thames & Hudson, 1981), "The Inkhuk Portfolio," pp. 110–27.

28 On VKhUTEMAS, see Khan-Magomedov, *Pioneers,* pp. 70–73, and A. Senkevitch, "Aspects of spatial form and perceptual psychology in the doctrine of the Rationalist movement in Soviet architecture of the 1920s," *VIA-6,* University of Pennsylvania, 1983, pp. 79–116.

29 For a brief memoir of her later student years, see Lidia Komarova, "A master from the people"; Gozak and Leonidov, *Ivan Leonidov,* pp. 26–27.

30 Adaskina and Sarabianov, *Lioubov Popova;* Alexander Lavrentiev, *Stepanova: A Constructivist Life* (London: Thames & Hudson, 1988).

31 S. M. Kirov, "Speech to the 1st Congress of Soviets," 20 December 1922. For this and other documents on the Palace of Labor competition, see V. Khazanova, comp., *Iz istorii sovetskoi arkhitektury 1917–1925: dokumenty i materialy* (From the History of Soviet Architecture 1917–1925: documents and materials) (Moscow: Nauka [Science], 1963), pp. 146–53.

32 Immediately after the Revolution, most art and architecture schools in Russia were reorganized into "Free Studios," or Svomas. In 1920 the Moscow Svomas became consolidated into the multi-disciplinary school called VKhUTEMAS (Higher Artistic and Technical Studios). In Petrograd, however, the "freedom" was considered by staff (and many students) too close to chaos, and the Svomas that had been created out of the Imperial Academy of Arts school reverted to being a formally organized Academy in 1921.

33 M. Ginzburg, "Itogi i perspektivy" (Achievements and prospects), *Sovremennaia arkhitektura* (Contemporary Architecture), 1927, no. 4/5, p. 116.

34 Several were illustrated by Ginzburg in his *Stil' i epokha* (Moscow: 1924); see M. Ginzburg, *Style and Epoch: Oppositions*/MIT Press, 1982), plates 1–7, 18–19. See also Starr, *Melnikov,* pp. 58–63.

35 K. Melnikov, "Arkhitektura moei zhizni" (The architecture of my life) (1967), ms., in A. A. Strigalev and I. V. Kokkinaki, eds., *Konstantin Stepanovich Melnikov,* (Moscow: Iskusstvo [Art], 1985), pp. 57–91.

36 Starr, *Melnikov,* pp. 81–84.

37 *Izvestiia,* 31 December 1924, in Khazanova, comp., *Iz istorii, 1917–1925,* pp. 227–29.

38 Competition report, quoted from archival sources in S. O. Khan-Magomedov, *Il'ia Golosov,* (Moscow: Stroi-izdat [Construction Publishers], 1988), p. 114.

39 *Sovremennaia arkhitektura* (Contemporary Architecture), 1926, no. 1, pp. 1–3.

40 The project is illustrated in Ginzburg, *Style and Epoch,* plates 14–16.

41 Archival documents of the committee, quoted in Khazanova, comp., *Iz istorii, 1917–1925,* p. 190.

42 Illustrated with numerous preliminary variants in Starr, *Melnikov,* chapter V, "International Debut." Further important data on the role of Rodchenko et al, in J.-L. Cohen, "Il padiglione di Mel'nikov a Parigi: una seconda ricostruzione," *Casabella* (Milan), November 1986, pp. 40–51.

43 I. Fomin, "Poiasnitel'noi zapiski k proektu paviliona SSSR v Parizhe" (Explanatory notes to the project for the USSR pavilion in Paris), archival documents quoted in Khazanova, comp., *Iz istorii 1917–1925*, pp. 187–88.

44 For a detailed account, see Zenovia A. Sochor, *Revolution and Culture: the Bogdanov-Lenin Controversy* (Ithaca, N.Y.: Cornell University Press, 1988).

45 V. I. Lenin, "Speech to the 3rd All-Russian Congress of the Komsomol," 2 October 1920, in *Collected Works* (Moscow: Progress Publishers, 1965), vol. 31, pp. 283–99.

46 Lenin, quoting Marx, in ibid.

47 Khan-Magomedov, *Pioneers*, pp. 198–99.

48 I. Fomin, "Arkhitektura Moskovskogo klassitsizma" (The architecture of Moscow classicism), *Mir iskusstva* (The World of Art), 1904, no. 7.

49 I. A. Fomin, "Tvorcheskie puti sovetskoi arkhitektury i problema arkhitekturnogo nasledstva" (The creative path of Soviet architecture and the problem of the architectural heritage), *Arkhitektura SSSR* (Architecture USSR), 1933, no. 3–4, pp. 15–16.

50 A. V. Shchusev, "Lektsiia: stroitel'stvo naselennikh mest" (Lecture: the construction of populated places), 1926, in M. G. Barkhin, ed., *Mastera sovetskoi arkhitektury ob arkhitekture* (Masters of Soviet architecture on architecture) (Moscow: Iskusstvo [Art], 1975), vol. 1, pp. 170–71.

51 V. A. Shchuko, "Tvorcheskii otchet" (Creative report), *Arkhitektura SSSR* (Architecture USSR), 1935, no. 6.

52 A. V. Lunacharsky, "Ob otdele izobrazitel'nikh iskusstv" (On the Fine Art section), 1920, in A. V. Lunacharsky, *Ob iskusstve* (On art) (Moscow: Iskusstvo [Art], 1982), vol. 2, pp. 79–83.

53 A. V. Lunacharsky, "Iskusstvo v Moskve" (Art in Moscow), speech to 3rd Congress of Comintern, July 1921, in Lunacharsky, *Ob iskusstve*, vol. 2, pp. 94–100.

54 Khan-Magomedov, *Pioneers*, section 4, pp. 106–45.

55 N. Ladovsky, "Osnovy postroeniia teorii arkhitektury: pod znakom rationalisticheskoi estetiki" (Foundations for building a theory of architecture: under the banner of rationalist aesthetics), *Izvestiia ASNOVA* (ASNOVA News), no. 1, 1926, pp. 3–5.

56 N. Ladovsky, "Iz protokolov zasedaniia kommissii zhiv-skulpt-arkha" (From minutes of meetings of the Commission for Paint-Sculpt-Architecture), 1919, archival material quoted in Barkhin, ed., *Mastera*, vol. 1, pp. 343–44.

57 Ladovsky, "Osnovy postroeniia teorii arkhitektury."

58 The best source on the Rationalists' work and theory is Senkevitch, "Aspects of spatial form and perceptual psychology."

59 N. Ladovsky, "Psikho-tekhnicheskaia laboratoriia arkhitektury" (The psychotechnical laboratory of architecture), *Izvestiia ASNOVA* (ASNOVA News), no. 1, 1926, p. 7.

60 Khan-Magomedov, *Pioneers*, section 5, pp. 146–56; Khan-Magomedov, *Rodchenko*; C. Cooke, "The development of the Constructivist architects' design method," in A. Papadakis, A. Benjamin, and C. Cooke, eds., *Deconstruction: Omnibus Volume* (New York: Rizzoli, 1989), pp. 21–37, and earlier version in *Architectural Design*, 1983, no. 5/6, pp. 34–49.

61 Ginzburg, *Style and Epoch*; on its intellectual origins and development of Ginzburg's earlier thinking, see A. Senkevitch, "Introduction: Moisei Ginzburg and the emergence of a Constructivist theory of architecture," ibid., pp. 10–33.

62 Letter from L. Vesnin, archival material quoted in A. G. Chiniakov, *Brat'ia Vesniny* (The Vesnin Brothers) (Moscow: Stroi-izdat [Construction Publishers], 1970), p. 99.

63 M. Ginzburg, "Novye metody arkhitekturnogo myshleniia" (New methods of architectural thinking), *Sovremennaia arkhitektura* (Contemporary Architecture), 1926, no. 1, pp. 1–8.

64 Ibid.

65 Cooke, "The development of the Constructivist architects' design method"; C. Cooke, "The machine as a model: the Russian Constructivists' conception of the design process," *Architectural Design*, 1989, no. 7/8, pp. XI–XV.

66 A. V. Lunacharsky, "Khudozhestvennoe tvorchestvo natsional'nostei SSSR" (Artistic creativity of the various Soviet nationalities), in G. A. Belaia, comp., *Iz istorii sovetskoi esteticheskoi mysli 1917–1932* (From the History of Soviet Aesthetic Thought 1917–1932) (Moscow: Iskusstvo [Art], 1980), pp. 85–87.

67 Ibid.

68 Starr, *Melnikov*, pp. 66–67; also documents in Strigalev and Kokkinaki, eds., *Konstantin Stepanovich Melnikov* (Moscow: Iskusstvo, 1985), pp. 92–94.

69 "Nakaz arkhitekturnogo izucheniia po programme masterskikh 'Novaia akademiia'" (Instructions for architectural study according to the program of studios in "The New Academy"), in Strigalev and Kokkinaki, eds., *Konstantin Stepanovich Melnikov*, pp. 93–94.

70 K. Melnikov, "Oformlenie proekta" (Design of the project), *Arkhitektura SSSR* (Architecture USSR), 1933, no. 5, p. 35; partially translated into English in Khan-Magomedov, *Pioneers*, pp. 551–52.

71 K. Melnikov, manuscript of 1965, family archives, Strigalev and Kokkinaki, eds., *Konstantin Stepanovich Melnikov*, pp. 239–40; partially translated in C. Cooke, "Moscow publishes the writings of Melnikov," *Architectural Design*, 1986, no. 4, pp. 4–5.

72 "Kredo" (Credo), undated ms., in Barkhin, ed., *Mastera*, vol. 2, p. 161.

73 Ms. notes from the early twenties in State Archives, translated in Khan-Magomedov, *Pioneers*, pp. 562–63.

74 A montage of the initial high-rise proposal and a photograph of the finished building were published in 1930 by El Lissitzky in his *Russland. Die Rekonstruktion der Arkhitektur in der Sowjetunion*, plates 40–42. See English-language edition, *Russia: An Architecture for World Revolution* (Cambridge, Mass.: MIT Press, 1970).

75 G. B. Barkhin, "Avtobiograficheskie zapiski" (Autobiographical notes), 1965, quoted in A. G. Barkhina, *G. B. Barkhin* (Moscow: Stroi-izdat [Construction Publishers], 1981), p. 122.

76 A. V. Shchusev, "Lektsiia: stroitel'stvo naselenikh mest."

77 A. Kopp, *Town and Revolution: Soviet Architecture and City Planning 1917–1935* (New York: George Braziller, 1970), pp. 126–55.

78 Quoted in S. O. Khan-Magomedov, "Psikhotekhnicheskaia laboratoriia VKhUTEINa, 1927–1930" (The psychotechnical laboratory of the VKhUTEIN, 1927–1930), *Tekhnicheskaia estetika* (Technical Aesthetics) (Moscow), 1978, no. 1, pp. 16–22. On Krutikov, see also Khan-Magomedov, *Pioneers*, pp. 282–83.

79 A. Mikhailov, *Gruppirovki sovetskoi arkhitektury* (The groupings of Soviet architecture) (Moscow-Leningrad: Ogiz, 1932), p. 110.

80 The project was given very full coverage in *Sovremennaia arkhitektura* (Contemporary Architecture), 1927, no. 4/5, from which facsimile pages are reproduced in Gozak and Leonidov, *Ivan Leonidov*, pp. 43–48.

81 Ginzburg, "Itogi i perspektivy," partially translated in Gozak and Leonidov, *Ivan Leonidov*, p. 42.

82 Various stages of this Vesnin project are illustrated in detail in A. Kopp, *Constructivist Architecture in the USSR* (New York: St. Martin's Press, 1985), pp. 52–57; the Fidman project appears on p. 58.

83 Andrei Leonidov, "Reminiscences of my father," in Gozak and Leonidov, *Ivan Leonidov*, pp. 21–25.

84 C. Cooke, "Russian Constructivism and the city," *UIA Journal of Theory and Criticism*, vol. 1, no. 1, 1988, pp. 16–25; Cooke, "The development of the Constructivist architects' design method," p. 31.

85 Leonidov's full commentary and extensive visual documentation on the "Club of New Social Type" concept appear in Gozak and Leonidov, *Ivan Leonidov*, pp. 60–67.

86 This project is documented in ibid, pp. 72–76.

87 G. Krutikov, "Voprosy prostranstvennoi organizatsii kul'turnogo kombinata" (Questions of the spatial organization of a cultural combine), *Stroitel'naia promyshlennost'* (The Building Industry) (Moscow), 1930, no. 10, p. 794; partially translated in ibid, p. 77.

88 A. Karra and V. Simbirtsev, "Forpost proletarskoi kul'tury" (The outpost of proletarian culture), *Stroitel'stvo Moskvy* (The Construction of Moscow), 1930, no. 8/9, p. 22; partially translated in ibid, p. 77.

89 A. Mordvinov, "Leonidovshchina i ego vred" (Leonidovism and the harm it does), *Iskusstvo v massy* (Art to the Masses), 1930, no. 12, pp. 12–15; translated in ibid, pp. 96–97.

90 On VOPRA, see Khan-Magomedov, *Pioneers*, pp. 236–38, 600–1.

91 On Chernikhov's Constructive work, see C. Cooke, *Chernikhov: Fantasy & Construction*, Architectural Design Profile no. 55 (New York: St. Martin's Press, 1984). On the totality of his oeuvre, see C. Cooke, ed., with A. Chernikhov, *Iakov Chernikhov's Architectural Fantasies*, Architectural Design Profile no. 80 (New York: St. Martin's Press, 1989).

92 On the background and development of this competition, see A. Cunliffe, "The competition for the Palace of Soviets in Moscow, 1931–1933," *Architectural Association Quarterly* (London) vol. 11, no. 2, 1979, pp. 36–48. For a recent Soviet account, see A. V. Riabushin, *Gumanizm sovetskoi arkhitektury* (The humanism of Soviet architecture) (Moscow: Stroi-izdat [Construction Publishers], 1986), pp. 135–55.

93 Competition program, paragraph 1, quoted in M. V. Kriukov, ed., *Biuleten' upravleniia stroitel'stvom Dvortsa Sovetov pri prezidiume TsIK SSSR* (Bulletin of the Palace of Soviets Construction Administration of the Presidium of the Central Committee of the Communist Party), Party Executive Committee of Moscow Oblast (Moscow), 1931, no. 2–3 (October), p 35; also "The construction of a Palace of Soviets in Moscow," *Soviet Culture Bulletin*, VOKS (Moscow), no. 2, July 1931.

94 I. Iu. Eigel', *Boris Iofan* (Moscow: Stroi-izdat, 1978).

95 L. Kaganovich, "O moskovskom gorodskom khoziaistve i o razvitii gorodskogo khoziaistva SSSR" (On the Moscow urban economy and on the development of the urban economy of the USSR), *Pravda* (Moscow), 4 July 1931, pp. 3–4.

96 M. V. Kriukov, ed., *Biuleten' upravleniia stroitel'stvom Dvortsa Sovetov*, no. 2–3, p. 1.

97 Ibid., pp. 47, 28.

98 Ibid., p. 8.

99 Ibid., p. 45.

100 Ibid., pp. 20–21.

101 Ibid., pp. 15, 13.

102 Ibid., p. 1.

103 Ibid., p. 1.

104 G. Barkhin, "Inostrannye arkhitektory na konkurse Dvortsa Sovetov" (Foreign architects in the competition for the Palace of Soviets), in *Dvorets Sovetov* (Palace of Soviets) (Moscow), 1933, pp. 81–87, quoted in Riabushin, *Gumanizm*, pp. 147–48.

105 N. p. Zapletin, "Dvorets sovetov SSSR" (The Palace of Soviets of the USSR), *Sovetskaia arkhitektura* (Soviet Architecture), 1932, no. 2–3, p. 10. Le Corbusier's scheme is illustrated in detail in *Le Corbusier: The Complete Architectural Works*, vol. II: 1929–1934, (London: Thames & Hudson, 1966), pp. 123–37. For background, discussion, and further documentation, see J.-L. Cohen, *Le*

Corbusier et la mystique, pp. 204–45, and S. Frederick Starr, "Le Corbusier and the USSR: new documentation," *Oppositions* (New York), no. 23, winter 1981, pp. 122–37. The other foreign projects are illustrated in "The Palace of Soviets, Moscow," *Architectural Review* (London), May 1932, pp. 196–200.

106 Published in *Pravda*, 24 April 1932. See V. Khazanova, comp., *Iz istorii sovetskoi arkhitektury 1926–32: dokumenty i materialy* (From the History of Soviet Architecture 1926–32: documents and materials) (Moscow: Nauka [Science], 1970), p. 163. For an English translation, see C. Vaughan James, *Soviet Socialist Realism: Origins and Theory* (London and New York: Macmillan, 1973), p. 120. Although itself aimed mainly at writers and literature, a clause resolving "to carry out an analogous change with regard to other forms of art" led the way to its extension into fields like architecture.

107 *Izvestiia*, 18 July 1932. The announcement reads: "A Union of Soviet Architects has been created. The following have been elected to the Board of the new Union: prof. V. A. Vesnin, architects K. S. Alabian, V. S. Balikhin, S. F. Babaev, prof. M. Ia. Ginzburg, academician-architect I. V. Zholtovsky, architect A. M. Zaslavsky, chairman of the central committee of the Union of Builders I. G. Kelin, architects M. A. Krutikov, N. A. Ladovsky, V. A. Markov, Urban, D. F. Fridman." Source: Khazanova, comp., *Iz istorii 1926–1932*, p. 163.

108 An excellent discussion appears in Vaughan James, *Soviet Socialist Realism*. One of its earliest usages in the architectural context was in I. Voblyi, "Dvorets sovetov i arkhitekturnoe nasledstvo" (The Palace of Soviets and the architectural heritage), *Brigada khudozhnikov* (Brigade of Artists), 1932, no. 3.

109 A. N. Tolstoi, "Poiski monumental'nosti" (The search for monumentality), *Izvestiia*, 27 February 1932.

110 N. p. Zapletin, "Dvorets sovetov SSSR."

111 N. p. Zapletin, "Magnitostroi arkhitektury" (The Magnitogorsk project of architecture), *Stroitel'stvo Moskvy* (The Construction of Moscow), 1933, no. 5–6, p. 10, quoted in Riabushin, *Gumanizm*, p. 149.

112 Iofan's project for this stage is illustrated in Cunliffe, "The Competition," p. 42.

113 For plans, models, and sections of Ginzburg's project, see Kopp, *Town and Revolution*, pp. 218–21 (captioning slightly incorrect).

114 This Iofan scheme is illustrated in Khan-Magomedov, *Pioneers*, fig. 1127, also in Cunliffe, "The competition," p. 44.

115 "O proekte dvortsa sovetov" (On the project for the Palace of Soviets), published in the Union of Architects' new official journal *Sovetskaia arkhitektura* (Soviet Architecture), 1933, no. 4, p. 1, and in *Stroitel'stvo Moskvy* (The Construction of Moscow), 1933, no. 5–6, p. 1.

116 "Ob organizatsii okonchatel'noi razrabotki proekta dvortsa sovetov" (On the organization of the final working out of the Palace of Soviets design), *Stroitel'stvo Moskvy* (The Construction of Moscow), 1933, no. 5–6, p. 2. I have not been able to identify the remaining few persons named.

117 "Ot zadaniia k proektu" (From brief to project), *Stroitel'stvo Moskvy* (The Construction of Moscow), 1934, no. 3, pp. 10–11. Kopp, *Town and Revolution*, p. 233, illustrates this project, but the caption is partially incorrect.

118 "Ob organizatsii okonchatel'noi razrabotki," p. 2.

119 Eigel', *Boris Iofan*, p. 99.

120 The character of this area of Moscow is described in C. Cooke, "Moscow Map Guide."

121 D. Aronovich, "Arkhitekturnaia rekonstruktsiia tsentra Moskvy" (The architectural reconstruction of the center of Moscow), *Stroitel'stvo Moskvy* (The Construction of Moscow), 1934, no. 10, pp. 20–29. A range of projects is illustrated in C. Cooke, "Ivan Leonidov: vision and historicism," *Architectural Design* (London), 1986, no. 6, pp. 12–21.

122 Editorial on the competition projects, *Arkhitektura SSSR* (Architecture USSR), 1934, no. 10, p. 4.

123 M. Ginzburg, "Amerika," *Sovremennaia arkhitektura* (Contemporary Architecture), 1926, no. 1, p. 38.

124 K. Melnikov, "Masterskaia no. 7" (Report of Studio no. 7), in *Sbornik rabot arkhitekturnykh masterskikh Mossoveta, 1934g* (Collection of works of the architectural studios of Mossoviet for the year 1934), reproduced in Strigalev and Kokkinaki, *Konstantin Stepanovich Melnikov*, pp. 217–18.

125 Starr, *Melnikov*, fig. 213, p. 195, reproduces the building's cross section.

126 K. Melnikov, "Poiasnitel'naia zapiska" (Explanatory note), *Arkhitektura SSSR* (Architecture USSR), 1934, no. 10, pp. 16–17.

127 Ibid.

128 L. Lisitskii (El Lissitzky), "Forum sotsialisticheskoi Moskvy" (A forum for socialist Moscow), *Arkhitektura SSSR* (Architecture USSR), 1934, no. 10, p. 5.

129 V. S. Balikhin, "Sintez iskusstv v praktike sovetskoi arkhitektury" (The synthesis of the arts in the practice of Soviet architecture), *Arkhitektura SSSR* (Architecture USSR), 1935, no. 7, p. 26.

130 A sketch indicating the main contextual elements appears in C. Cooke, "Ivan Leonidov," p. 19.

131 Leonidov's montage onto an old print is illustrated in C. Cooke, "Ivan Leonidov," p. 18, and Gozak and Leonidov, *Ivan Leonidov*, p. 114.

132 Gozak and Leonidov, *Ivan Leonidov*, pp. 12, 110.

133 For further discussion of this theme, see C. Cooke, "Ivan Leonidov."

134 Lisitskii, "Forum sotsialisticheskoi Moskvy."

135 Editorial on the competition projects, *Arkhitektura SSSR* (Architecture USSR), 1934, no. 10, p. 4.

Plates

1 Vladimir Shchuko
*Monument to the Victims of the Revolution
in Helsinki*
Unexecuted
Petrograd (?), 1917
Perspective
Colored pencil and charcoal on paper
9 × 9½" (23 × 24 cm)

Opposite:
2 Nikolai Kolli
*Decorations for the First Anniversary of the
October Revolution—"The Red Wedge"*
Executed project
Moscow, 1918
Perspective
Pencil, watercolor, and ink on paper
13 × 8⅛" (33 × 20.5 cm)

Утверждено рада

БАНДЫ

КРАСНОВА

3 Vladimir Krinsky
Formal Composition
1920
Pencil on paper
8¼ × 5⅞″ (21 × 15 cm)

4 Vladimir Krinsky
Formal Composition
1919
Pencil, watercolor, and ink on paper
9⅞ × 5⅝″ (25.1 × 14.2 cm)

Right:
5 Vladimir Krinsky
Formal Composition
Early 1920s
Watercolor, ink, and pencil on paper
3⅛ × 2½″ (8 × 6.5 cm)

СТЕКЛЯННОЕ ПОКРЫТИЕ

СТЕКЛЯННОЕ ПОКРЫТИЕ

ПЛАН

ВХОД

РАЗРЕЗ

ФАСАД

ВХОД

Вл. Кринский

7 Vladimir Krinsky
Temple of Communion between Nations
Experimental project (Zhivskulptarkh),
unexecuted
1919
Floor plan, perspective
Ink and watercolor on paper
6½ × 4½″ (16.5 × 11.5 cm)

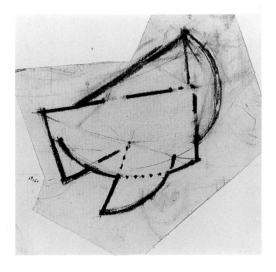

8 Vladimir Krinsky
Communal House
Experimental project (Zhivskulptarkh),
unexecuted
1920
Perspective
Ink, watercolor, and pencil on double tracing
paper
4⅜ × 5½" (11 × 14 cm)

9 Vladimir Krinsky
Communal House
Experimental project (Zhivskulptarkh),
unexecuted
1920
Floor plan
Pencil on paper
4½ × 4½" (11.5 × 11.5 cm)

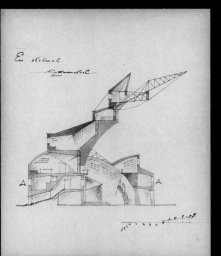

10 Nikolai Ladovsky
Communal House
Experimental project (Zhivskulptarkh),
unexecuted
1920
Elevation
Pencil, colored pencil, and colored ink on
tracing paper
15¾ × 12¼″ (40 × 31 cm)

11 Nikolai Ladovsky
Communal House
Experimental project (Zhivskulptarkh),
unexecuted
1920
Cross-section
Ink and pencil on paper
15⅜ × 12⅜″ (39 × 31.3 cm)

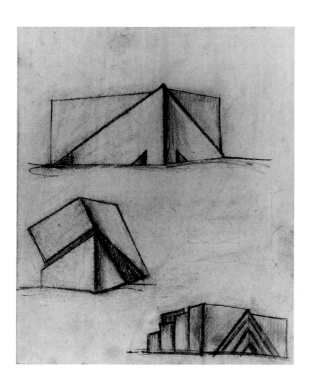

12 Ivan Lamtsov
*Student Assignment on the Manifestation
of Form*
(VKhUTEMAS, studio of N. A. Ladovsky)
Moscow, 1921
Pencil on paper
9 × 7¼″ (23 × 18.4 cm)

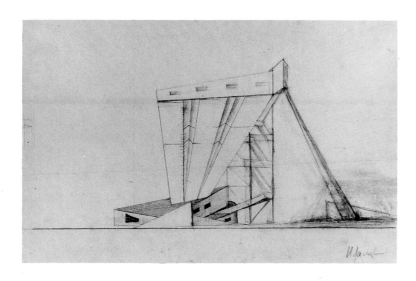

Above:
13 Ivan Lamtsov
*Student Assignment on the Manifestation
of Form*
(VKhUTEMAS, studio of N. A. Ladovsky)
Moscow, 1921–22
Pencil on paper
6⅞ × 8¾″ (17.5 × 22.4 cm)

14 Ivan Lamtsov
Student Assignment Based on a Grain Elevator
(VKhUTEMAS, studio of N. A. Ladovsky)
Moscow, 1922
Perspective
Pencil on paper
8¼ × 13″ (21 × 33 cm)

15 Ivan Lamtsov
*Student Assignment on the Expression
of Mass and Weight*
(VKhUTEMAS, studio of N. A. Ladovsky)
Moscow, 1922
Perspective
Pencil on paper
11¾ × 8⅞″ (30 × 22.5 cm)

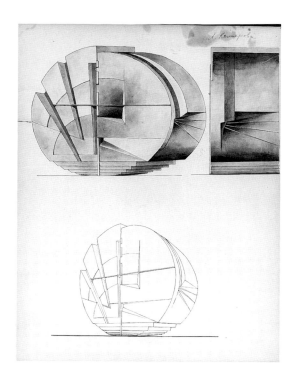

16 Lidia Komarova
*Student Assignment on the Demonstration
of Mass and Weight*
Early 1920s
Ink on paper
28 × 20⅞″ (71 × 53 cm)

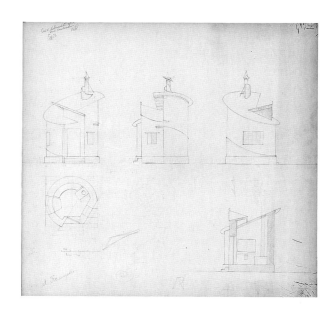

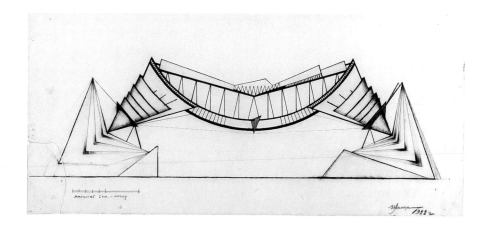

Above:
17 Lidia Komarova
Trackwalker's House
Student Assignment (VKhUTEMAS)
1923
Floor plan, cross-section, elevation
Pencil on paper
17¾ × 19¼″ (45 × 49 cm)

18 Ivan Lamtsov
*Student Assignment "Beam on Two Points
of Support"*
(VKhUTEMAS, studio of N. A. Ladovsky)
1922
Elevation
Cardboard, ink, charcoal, and pencil on paper
11¾ × 25¼″ (30 × 64 cm)

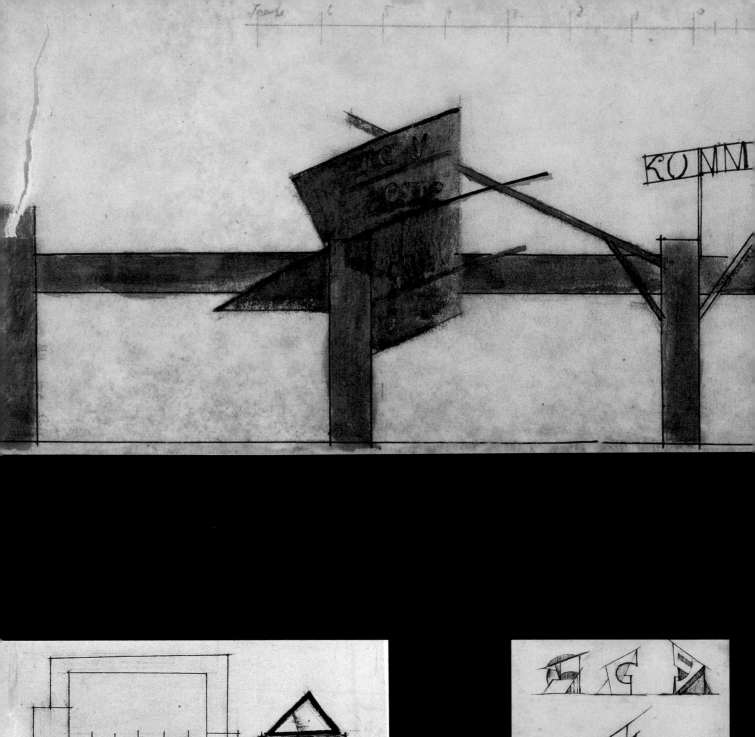
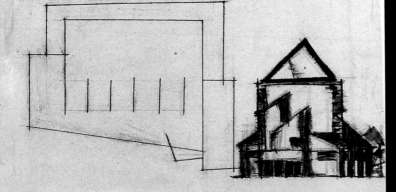
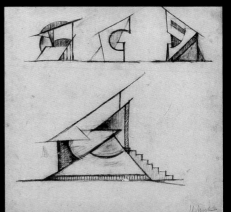

ПАВИЛЬОН
ДАЛЬНЯГО ВОСТОКА
БОКОВОЙ ФАСАД

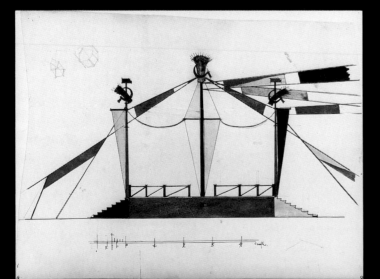

22 Ilia Golosov
Pavilion of a Far-Eastern Republic, for the All-
Russian Agricultural and Handicraft Industries
Exhibition, Moscow
Executed
Moscow, 1923
Elevation
Cardboard, watercolor, ink, and varnish on
paper
17 × 29½″ (43 × 75 cm)

23 Georgi Golts
Rostrum, for the All-Russian Agricultural and
Handicraft Industries Exhibition, Moscow
Unexecuted
Moscow, 1923
Elevation
Ink, watercolor, and bronze powder on paper
11¾ × 15⅝″ (30 × 39 cm)

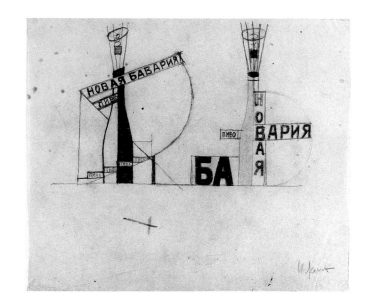

Above:
24 Ivan Lamtsov
"New Bavaria" Beer Kiosk, for the All-Russian
Agricultural and Handicraft Industries
Exhibition, Moscow
Unexecuted
Moscow, 1923
Elevations
Pencil and colored pencil on tracing paper
6⅞ × 8⅛″ (17.5 × 20.5 cm)

25 Anatoli Samoilov
Kiosk for Selling Perfumes
Unexecuted
Leningrad, early 1920s
Elevation
Ink, watercolor, and collage on paper
19¾ × 26⅜″ (50 × 67 cm)

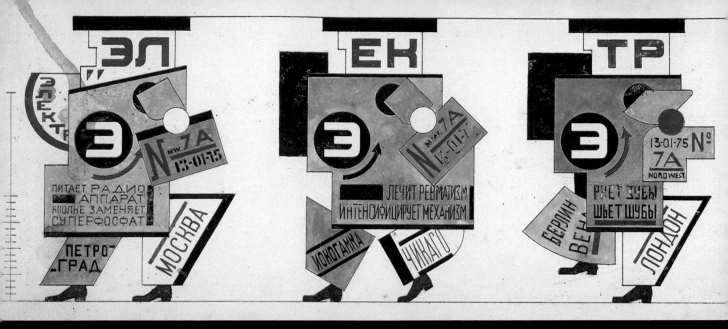

[30–34] Alexander Vesnin
Sets for the production "The Man Who Was Thursday" by G. K. Chesterton
Kamernyi Theater, Moscow, 1922–23
Director: Alexander Tairov
Sequence of sets throughout the performance

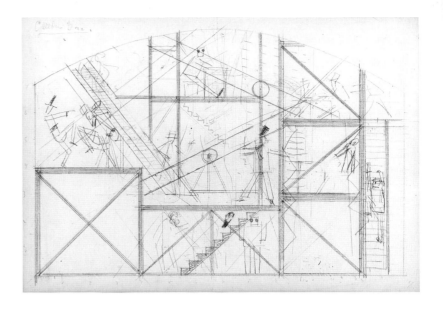

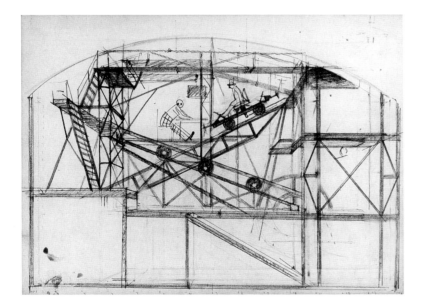

30 Pencil on paper, 10⅜ × 15⅜″ (26.5 × 39 cm)

31 Pencil on paper, 7¾ × 10⅞″ (19.8 × 27.8 cm)

32 Pencil on paper, 7⅞ × 10¼″ (19.9 × 26.1 cm)

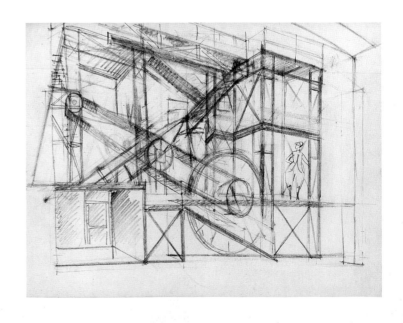

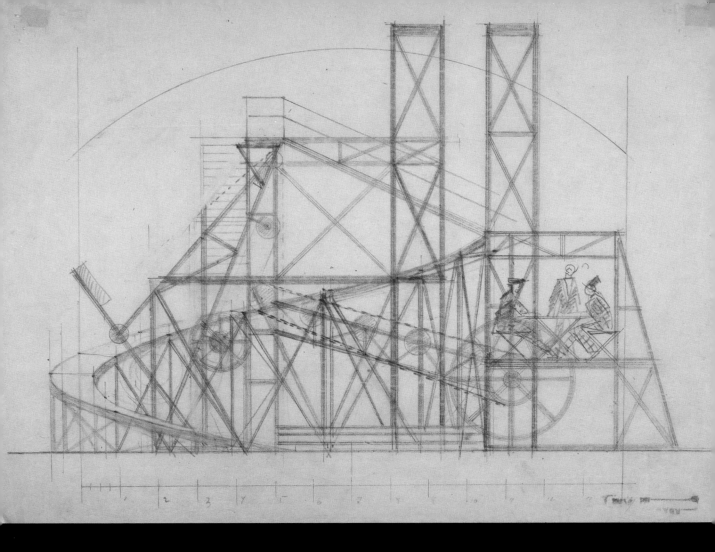

33 Pencil on tracing paper, 8⅞ × 12⅛″
(22.6 × 30.8 cm)

34 Pencil on tracing paper, 9⅛ × 10¾″
(23.3 × 27.3 cm)

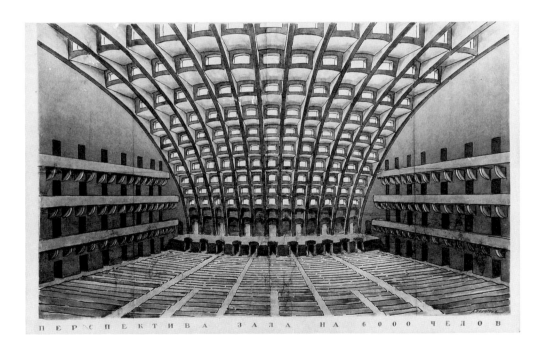

ПЕРСПЕКТИВА ЗАЛА НА 6000 ЧЕЛОВ

35 Andrei Belogrud
Palace of Labor
Competition project, unexecuted
Moscow, 1922–23
Exterior perspective
Pencil and colored ink on paper
26¾ × 50″ (68 × 127 cm)

36 Andrei Belogrud
Palace of Labor
Competition project, unexecuted
Moscow, 1922–23
Interior. Perspective of auditorium
Sepia on paper
27½ × 42¾″ (70 × 108.5 cm)

37 Alexander, Leonid, and Viktor Vesnin
Palace of Labor
Competition project, third prize, unexecuted
Moscow, 1922–23
Perspective
Pencil on tracing paper
17⅝ × 23¼″ (44.6 × 59.2 cm)

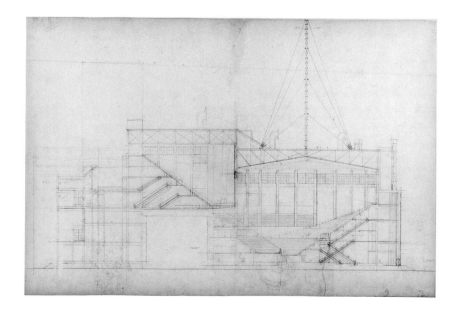

38 Alexander, Leonid, and Viktor Vesnin
Palace of Labor
Competition project, third prize, unexecuted
Moscow, 1922–23
Perspective sketch
Pencil on tracing paper
6⅝ × 8¼" (16.8 × 21 cm)

39 Alexander, Leonid, and Viktor Vesnin
Palace of Labor
Competition project, third prize, unexecuted
Moscow, 1922–23
Section
Pencil on tracing paper
16 × 23½" (40.6 × 59.8 cm)

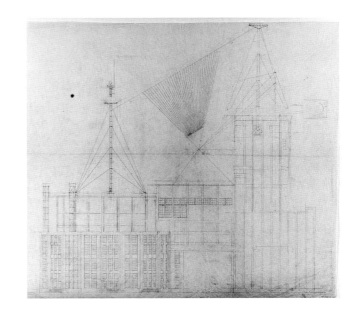

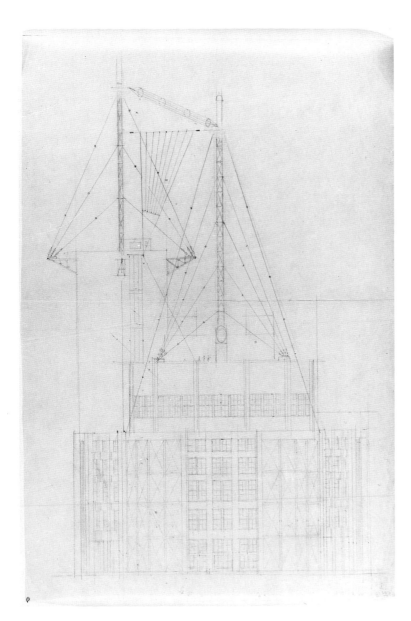

40 Alexander, Leonid, and Viktor Vesnin
Palace of Labor
Competition project, third prize, unexecuted
Moscow, 1922–23
Elevation
Pencil on tracing paper
20⅞ × 23⅝″ (53 × 60 cm)

41 Alexander, Leonid, and Viktor Vesnin
Palace of Labor
Competition project, third prize, unexecuted
Moscow, 1922–23
Elevation
Pencil on tracing paper
18⅞ × 12⅝″ (48 × 32 cm)

42 Alexander Gegello
Moscow Office of the Anglo-Russian Trading Company, ARCOS
Competition project, unexecuted
Moscow, 1924
Perspective
Ink and watercolor on paper
25⅝ × 31½″ (65 × 80 cm)

43 Alexander Gegello
Moscow Office of the Anglo-Russian Trading Company, ARCOS
Competition project, unexecuted
Moscow, 1924
Entrance elevation
Ink and watercolor on paper
17⅞ × 21½″ (45.5 × 54.5 cm)

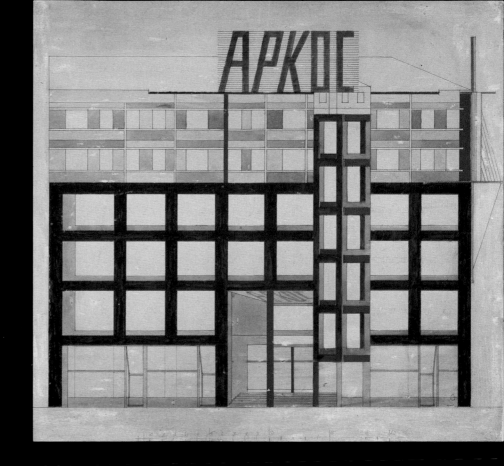

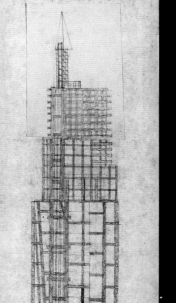

44 Vladimir Krinsky
*Moscow Office of the Anglo-Russian Trading
Company, ARCOS*
Competition project, unexecuted
Moscow, 1924
Entrance elevation
Paper on cardboard, ink, and gouache
14½ × 15⅜″ (37 × 39 cm)

45 Vladimir Krinsky
*Headquarters Building for the Council of the
National Economy, Vesenkha*
Experimental project, unexecuted
Moscow, 1922–23
Elevation
Pencil and colored pencil on tracing paper
12 × 5⅛″ (30.5 × 13 cm)

46 Konstantin Melnikov
Moscow Bureau of the Newspaper
"Leningrad Pravda"
Competition project, unexecuted
Moscow, 1924
Elevation showing each floor rotated to its
maximum extension
Ink on paper
26⅝×20″ (67.5×51 cm)

47 Alexander and Viktor Vesnin
Moscow Bureau of the Newspaper
"Leningrad Pravda"
Competition project, unexecuted
Moscow, 1924
Perspective
Pencil on paper
27³⁄₄ × 14¹⁄₄" (70.5 × 36 cm)

48 Ivan Fomin
USSR Pavilion, for the 1925 Exposition des Arts
Décoratifs, Paris
Competition project, unexecuted
Moscow, 1924
Perspective
Ink and colored ink on paper
21⅝ × 32⅞″ (55 × 83.5 cm)

50 Ilia Golosov
The Lenin House of the People, in Ivanovo-
Voznesensk (now Ivanovo)
Competition project, unexecuted
Moscow, 1924
Perspective
Board, ink, and gouache on paper
12⅝ × 24¾″ (32 × 63 cm)

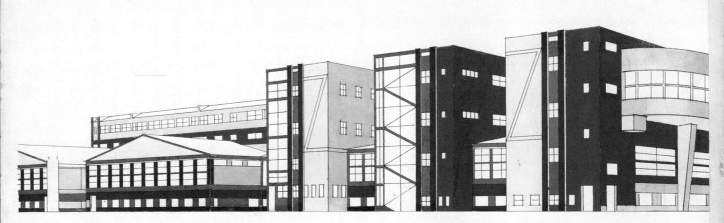

Electrobank Building, Moscow
Unexecuted
Moscow, 1926
Perspective
Ink and gouache on paper
26¾ × 38¾″ (68 × 98.5 cm)

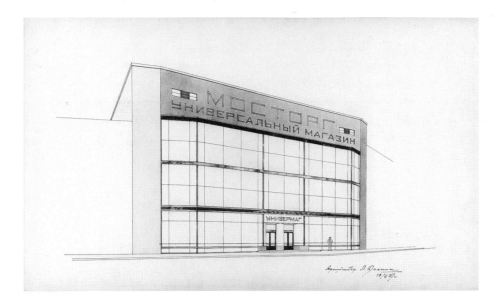

52 Alexander and Leonid Vesnin
Mostorg Department Store, Krasnaia Presnia,
Moscow
Executed
Moscow, 1925–27
Perspective
Ink, bronze powder, and watercolor on paper
16⅛ × 27¼″ (41 × 69 cm)

53 Viktor Vesnin
*Headquarters Building for the Agricultural
Bank, Ivselbank,* in Ivanovo-Voznesensk (now
Ivanovo)
Executed
Moscow, 1926–27
Perspective
Ink, bronze powder, and gray pastel on paper
20⅛ × 24⅜″ (51 × 62 cm)

Opposite:
54 Grigori and Mikhail Barkhin
Headquarters of the Newspaper "Izvestiia"
Executed
Moscow, 1926–27
Perspective
Ink, watercolor, and white ink on paper
37 × 22½″ (94 × 57 cm)

ЛЕНИН

Opposite:
55 Alexei Shchusev
Lenin Mausoleum
First version of the final project
Moscow, 1929–30
Floor plan, facade, perspective
Ink and gouache on paper
34⅝ × 26¼″ (87.4 × 66.7 cm)

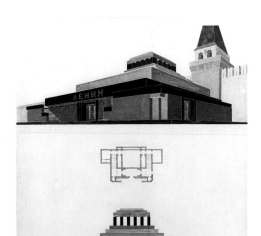

56 Ivan Fomin
Monument to Iakov Sverdlov
Competition project, unexecuted
Moscow, 1924
Elevation
Ink and charcoal on paper
27 × 22¼″ (68.5 × 56.6 cm)

57 Alexei Shchusev
Lenin Mausoleum
Executed version
Moscow, 1929–30
Floor plan, facade, perspective
Ink and gouache on paper
31½ × 26″ (80 × 66 cm)

58 Alexei Shchusev
Central Telegraph Building, Moscow
Competition project, unexecuted
Moscow, 1925
Perspective
Ink, gouache, white ink, and bronze powder
on paper on plywood
24 × 35⅞" (61 × 91 cm)

59 Mikhail and Adolf Minkus
House of Textiles
Competition project, unexecuted
Moscow, 1926
Perspective
Ink and colored ink on paper
27¼ × 22⅞" (69 × 58 cm)

Opposite:
60 Alexei Shchusev
Government Center for Samarkand
Unexecuted
Moscow, 1929–30
Perspective
Cardboard, charcoal, ink, gouache, and white
ink on gray paper
20⅞ × 14⅛" (53 × 36 cm)

ДОМ
ПРАВИТЕЛЬСТВА
в САМАРКАНДЕ

61 Mikhail Motylev
Workers' Housing, on Boevskaia and
Matrosskaia streets, Moscow
Executed
Moscow, 1927
Perspective, facades
Ink, gouache, and collage on paper
16⅛ × 22″ (41 × 56 cm)

Opposite, above:
62 Alexander Gegello
Cottage Housing Complex for Workers
Unexecuted
Leningrad, 1923
Elevations
Ink and watercolor on paper
10¼ × 37¾″ (26 × 96 cm)

Opposite, below:
63 Mikhail Motylev
Workers' Housing, on Novo-Riazanskaia Street,
Moscow
Executed
Moscow, 1927
Perspective
Ink and gouache on paper
13⅜ × 23⅝″ (34 × 60 cm)

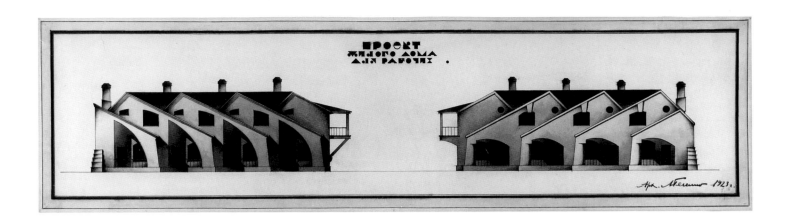

ПРОЕКТ
ЖИЛОГО ДОМА
ДЛЯ РАБОЧИХ.

Арх. Мешков 1923 г.

СОКСТРОЙ 1927 г.
РЯЗАНСКАЯ УЛ.
ВАРИАНТ-2

Moscow, 1928
Perspective
Ink, gouache, white ink, and collage on paper
34¼ × 95¾" (87 × 243 cm)

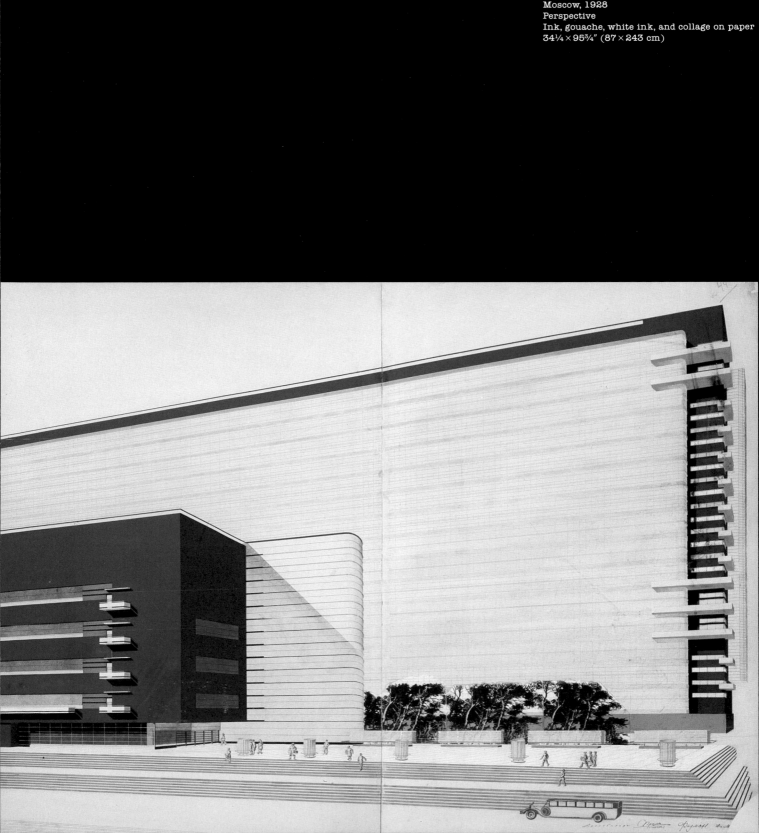

65 Alexander, Leonid, and Viktor Vesnin
Lenin State Public Library
Commissioned project, first version, unexecuted
Moscow, 1928
Perspective of main facade
Ink on paper
26⅜ × 39″ (67 × 99 cm)

66 Alexander, Leonid, and Viktor Vesnin
Lenin State Public Library
Commissioned project, second version, unexecuted
Moscow, 1928
Perspective of inner courtyard
Ink on paper
11½ × 17″ (29 × 43 cm)

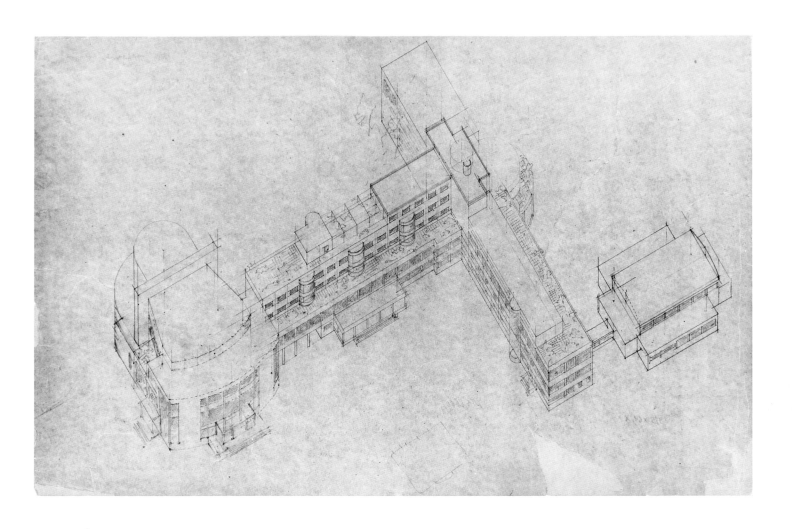

67 Alexander, Leonid, and Viktor Vesnin
*Palace of Culture of the Proletarsky District
(now the Likhachev Automobile Factory Club)*
Commissioned project, partially executed
Moscow, 1931–37
Axonometric
Pencil on tracing paper
15⅜ × 24¼" (39 × 61.5 cm)

68 Alexander, Leonid, and Viktor Vesnin
*Palace of Culture of the Proletarsky District
(now the Likhachev Automobile Factory Club)*
Commissioned project, partially executed
Moscow, 1931–37
Interior. Perspective of auditorium
Pencil on paper
11¾ × 16⅛" (30 × 41 cm)

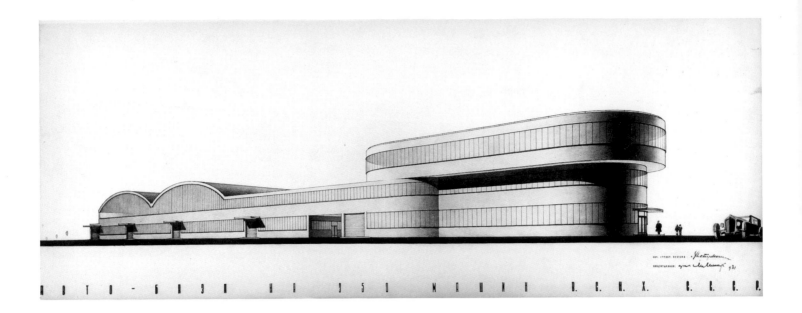

69 Mikhail Minkus
350-Car Garage
Unexecuted
Moscow, 1931
Perspective
Ink on paper
19¼ × 50¾″ (49 × 129 cm)

70 Panteleimon Golosov
*Printing Plant and Publishing Center
of the Newspaper "Pravda"*
Executed
Moscow, 1930–35
Perspective
Ink, watercolor, and white ink on paper
36¼ × 76¾″ (92 × 195 cm)

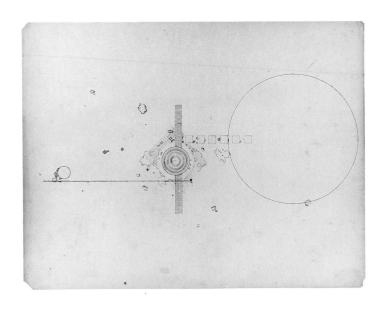

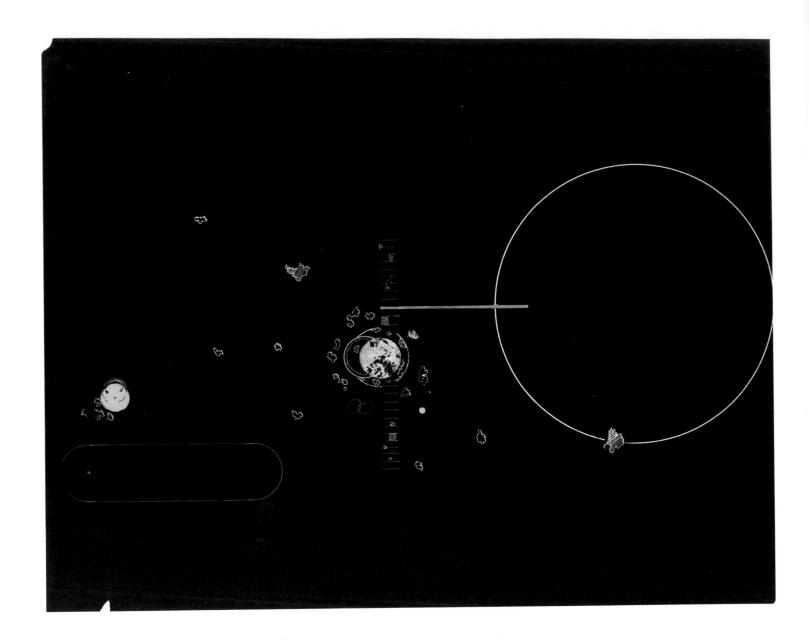

72 Ivan Leonidov
Club of New Social Type. Sports Pavilion
Experimental project, unexecuted. Variant B
1928
Ground-level plan
White ink and applied color on black paper
9¼ × 7⅛″ (23.5 × 18 cm)

73 Ivan Leonidov
Club of New Social Type. Sports Pavilion
Experimental project, unexecuted. Variant B
1928
First-floor plan
Ink on paper
7¼ × 9¼″ (18.5 × 23.5 cm)

74 Ivan Leonidov
Club of New Social Type. Sports Pavilion
Experimental project, unexecuted. Variant B
1928
Elevation
Ink on paper
7⅛ × 9¼″ (18.3 × 23 cm)

75 Ivan Leonidov
Club of New Social Type. Sports Pavilion
Experimental project, unexecuted. Variants A
and B
1928
Ground-level plan
Ink and applied color on paper
7⅛ × 9¼″ (18 × 23.5 cm)

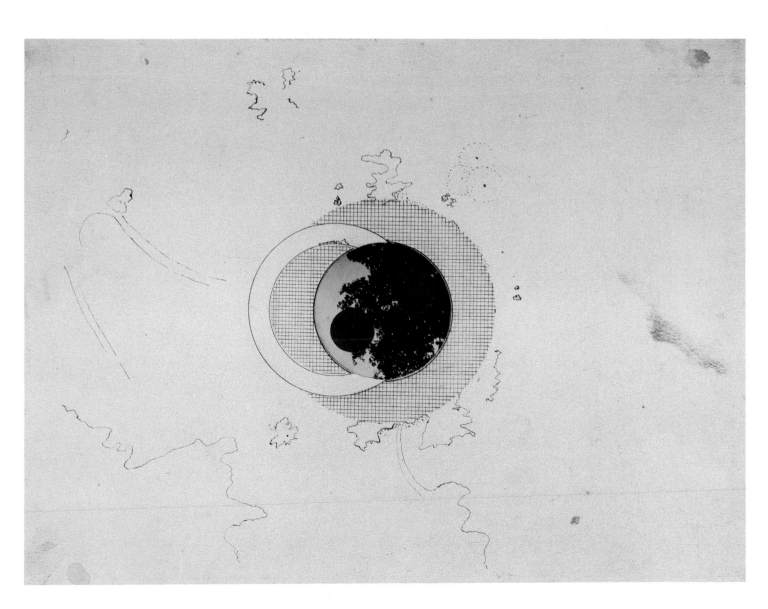

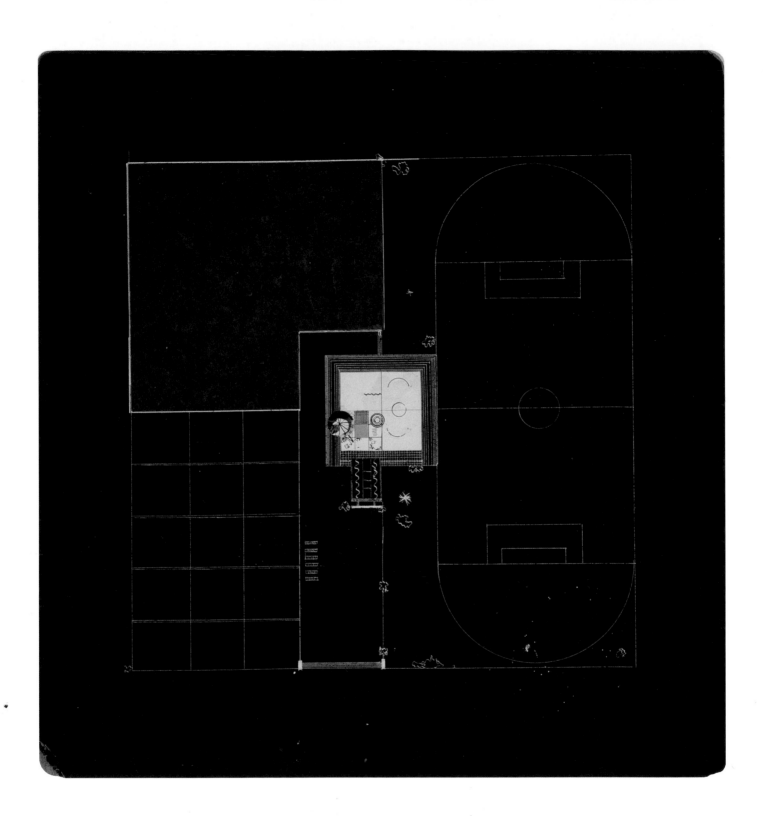

Opposite:
76 Ivan Leonidov
*Palace of Culture of the Proletarsky District of
Moscow. Center for Physical Education*
Competition project, first round, unexecuted
Moscow, 1930
Overall plan at ground level
Cardboard, white ink, and applied color on
black paper
13¾ × 13″ (35 × 33 cm)

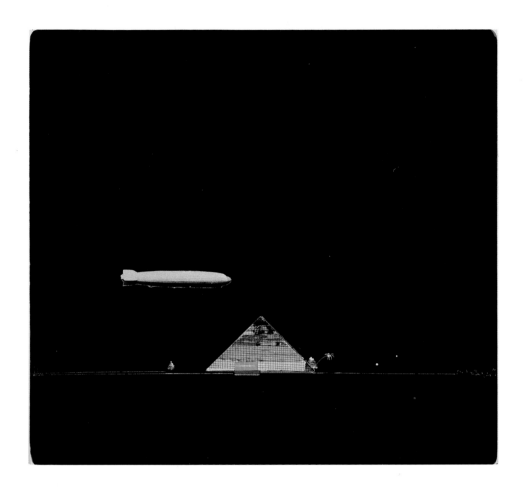

77 Ivan Leonidov
*Palace of Culture of the Proletarsky District of
Moscow. Center for Physical Education*
Competition project, first stage, unexecuted
Moscow, 1930
Elevation
Cardboard, white ink, and applied color on
black paper
13 × 13¾″ (33 × 35 cm)

78 Ivan Leonidov
*Palace of Culture of the Proletarsky District of
Moscow. Mass Activities Section*
Competition project, first stage, unexecuted
Moscow, 1930
Elevation
Black paper on cardboard, white ink, and
applied color
13¾ × 13″ (35 × 33 cm)

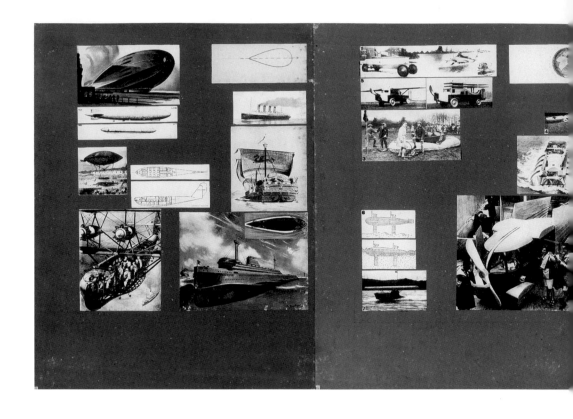

Above:
79 Georgi Krutikov
Flying City (literally "City on the Aerial Paths
of Communication")
Graduation work, unexecuted
(VKhUTEMAS, studio of N. A. Ladovsky)
Moscow, 1928
Collaged panels illustrating the theme "The
Evolution of the Mobile Home"
Cardboard, collage, pencil, and colored pencil on
gray paper
19 × 56¼" (48 × 143 cm)

Below:
80 Georgi Krutikov
Flying City
Graduation work, unexecuted
(VKhUTEMAS, studio of N. A. Ladovsky)
Moscow, 1928
Collaged panels illustrating the theme "Man's
Mastery of the Cosmic Atmosphere
Surrounding the Earth"
Gray paper, cardboard, and collage
19 × 56¼" (48 × 143 cm)

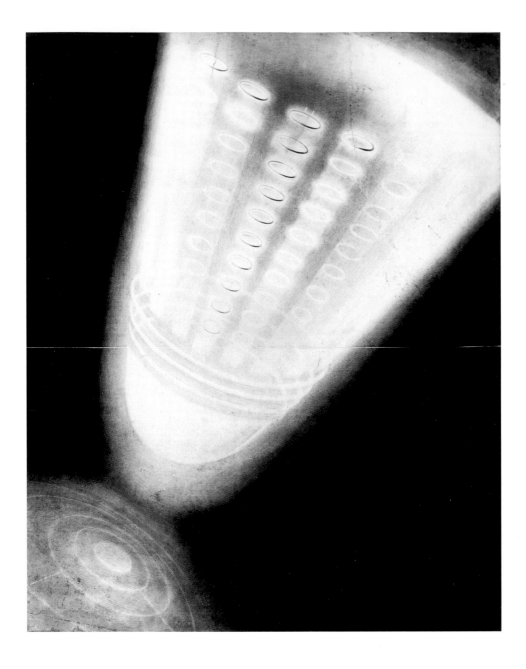

81 Georgi Krutikov
Flying City
Graduation work, unexecuted
(VKhUTEMAS, studio of N. A. Ladovsky)
Moscow, 1928
City perspective
Charcoal and pencil on paper
47¼ × 37″ (120 × 94 cm)

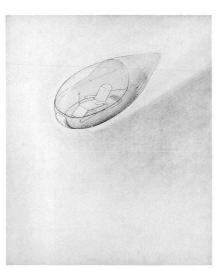

82 Georgi Krutikov
Flying City
Graduation work, unexecuted
(VKhUTEMAS, studio of N. A. Ladovsky)
Moscow, 1928
Flying cabin unit, perspective
Pencil, ink, and white ink on paper
45½ × 36¾″ (115.5 × 93.5 cm)

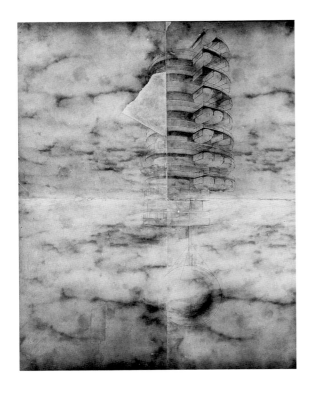

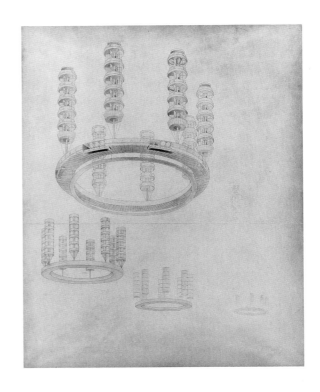

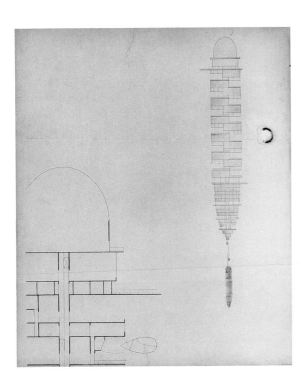

83 Georgi Krutikov
Flying City
Graduation work, unexecuted
(VKhUTEMAS, studio of N. A. Ladovsky)
Moscow, 1928
Apartment house-commune, perspective
Ink and pencil on photographic paper
45⅛ × 34⅝″ (114.5 × 88 cm)

Below:
84 Georgi Krutikov
Flying City
Graduation work, unexecuted
(VKhUTEMAS, studio of N. A. Ladovsky)
Moscow, 1928
Apartment complex, perspective
Pencil and ink on paper
45⅛ × 34⅝″ (114.5 × 88 cm)

85 Georgi Krutikov
Flying City
Graduation work, unexecuted
(VKhUTEMAS, studio of N. A. Ladovsky)
Moscow, 1928
Dwelling structure with hundreds of units
Detail of cross-section, elevation
Ink and pencil on paper
45¼ × 37¼″ (115 × 94.5 cm)

86 Nikolai Sokolov
Health-Resort Hotel
(VKhUTEMAS, studio of A. A. Vesnin)
Unexecuted project
Moscow, 1928
Perspective of the rural cabins
Ink, watercolor, gouache, and white ink on
paper
21½ × 14¼" (54.5 × 36 cm)

87 Nikolai Sokolov
Health-Resort Hotel
(VKhUTEMAS, studio of A. A. Vesnin)
Unexecuted project
Moscow, 1928
Explanatory panel of floor plans, elevations,
axonometrics, details
Ink, colored ink, white ink, and collage on
paper
21⅞ × 34⅝" (55.5 × 88 cm)

88 Nikolai Sokolov
Health-Resort Hotel
(VKhUTEMAS, studio of A. A. Vesnin)
Unexecuted project
Moscow, 1928
Axonometric
Ink, watercolor, gouache, and white ink on

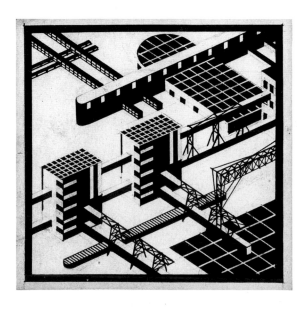

91 Iakov Chernikhov
Industrial Vignette, for the book *Architectural Fantasies: 101 Compositions* (Leningrad, 1933).
1928–31
Gouache on paper
4⅛ × 4⅛″ (10.5 × 10.5 cm)

92 Iakov Chernikhov
Industrial Vignette, for the book *Architectural Fantasies: 101 Compositions* (Leningrad, 1933)
1928–31
Gouache on paper
4¼ × 4¼″ (10.7 × 10.7 cm)

Opposite:
93 Iakov Chernikhov
Architectural Fantasy, published as Composition 75 in the book *Architectural Fantasies: 101 Compositions* (Leningrad, 1933)
1928–31
Ink and gouache on paper
12¼ × 9⅞″ (31 × 25 cm)

89 Iakov Chernikhov
Industrial Vignette, for the book *Architectural Fantasies: 101 Compositions* (Leningrad, 1933)
1928–31
Gouache on paper
4⅛ × 4⅛″ (10.5 × 10.5 cm)

90 Iakov Chernikhov
Industrial Vignette, for the book *Architectural Fantasies: 101 Compositions* (Leningrad, 1933)
1928–31
Ink and white ink on paper
4⅜ × 4⅜″ (11.2 × 11.2 cm)

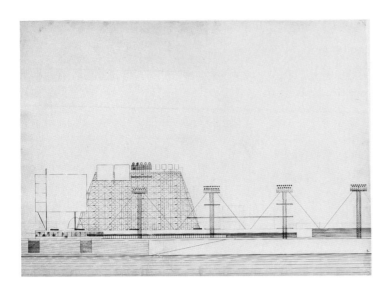

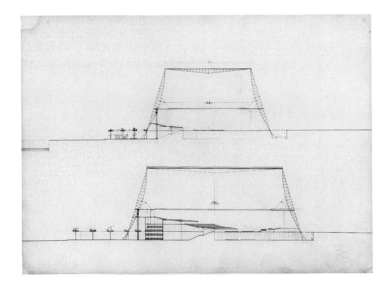

96 Team from ARU (Union of Architects and Urbanists): Nikolai Beseda, Georgi Krutikov, Vitali Lavrov, Valentin Popov, and Alexander Deineka (artist)
Palace of Soviets
Competition project, first (preliminary) stage, unexecuted
Moscow, February–May 1931
General site plan
Pencil, ink, gouache, white ink, and photographs on paper
45¼ × 45¼″ (115 × 115 cm)

Opposite:
97 Team from ARU (Union of Architects and Urbanists): Nikolai Beseda, Georgi Krutikov, Vitali Lavrov, Valentin Popov, and Alexander Deineka (artist)
Palace of Soviets
Competition project, first (preliminary) stage, unexecuted
Moscow, February–May 1931
Perspective
Ink, gouache, and white ink on paper
46½ × 46½″ (118 × 118 cm)

94 Team from SASS (Sector of Architects for Socialist Construction), formerly OSA:
Leonid Pavlov and Mikhail Kuznetsov
Palace of Soviets
Competition project, first (preliminary) stage, unexecuted
Moscow, February–May 1931
Facade
Ink and pencil on paper
24¼ × 34⅛″ (61.5 × 86.5 cm)

95 Team from SASS (Sector of Architects for Socialist Construction, formerly OSA):
Leonid Pavlov and Mikhail Kuznetsov
Palace of Soviets
Competition project, first (preliminary) stage, unexecuted
Moscow, February–May 1931
Cross-sections
Ink and pencil on paper
24⅜ × 34⅛″ (62 × 86.5 cm)

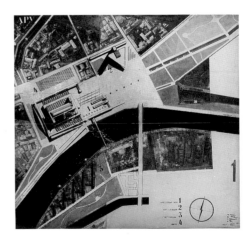

98 Designers unknown
Pseudonym: "The Red Building of the Soviets"
Palace of Soviets
Competition project, second (open) stage,
unexecuted
Moscow, February–May 1931
Floor plan, cross-section, axonometrics
Ink, white ink, and collage on paper
28½ × 41″ (72.5 × 104 cm)

99 Alexander Karra
Palace of Soviets
Competition project, second (open) stage,
unexecuted
Moscow, July–December 1931
Axonometric view into auditorium
Ink on paper
27⅜ × 21¾" (69.5 × 55 cm)

100 Alexander Karra
Palace of Soviets
Competition project, second (open) stage,
unexecuted
Moscow, July–December 1931
Axonometric
Ink on paper
26 × 36¼" (66 × 92 cm)

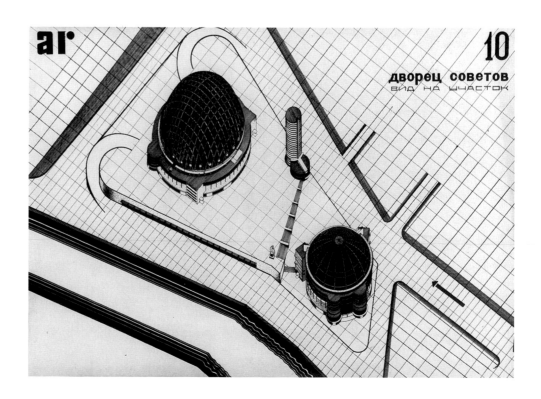

161 Moisei Ginzburg, Gustav Gassenpflug, and Solomon Lisagor
Palace of Soviets
Competition project, third stage, unexecuted
Moscow, March–July 1932
Facade
Ink, watercolor, and white ink on paper
26¾ × 74¾" (68 × 190 cm)

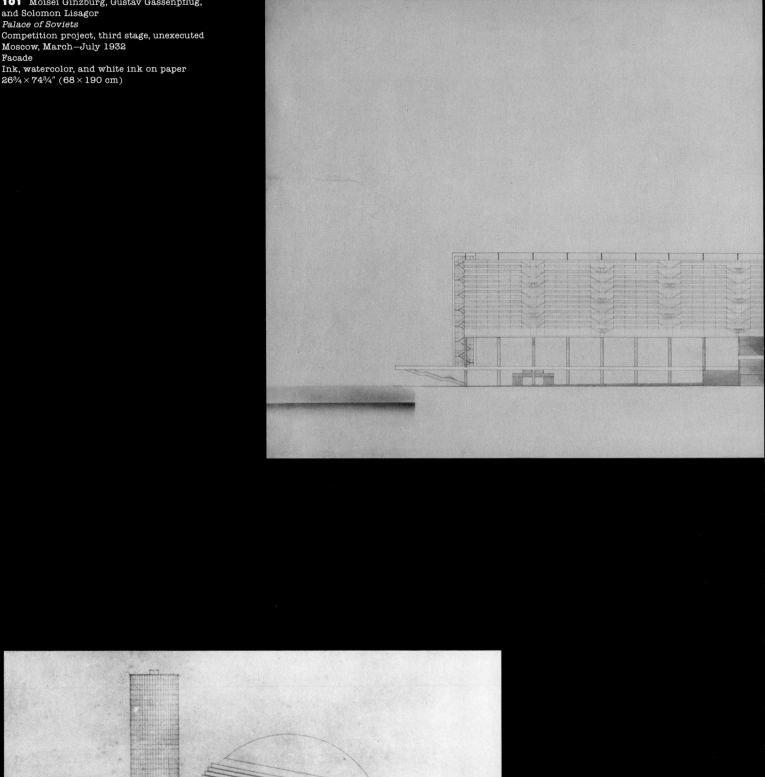

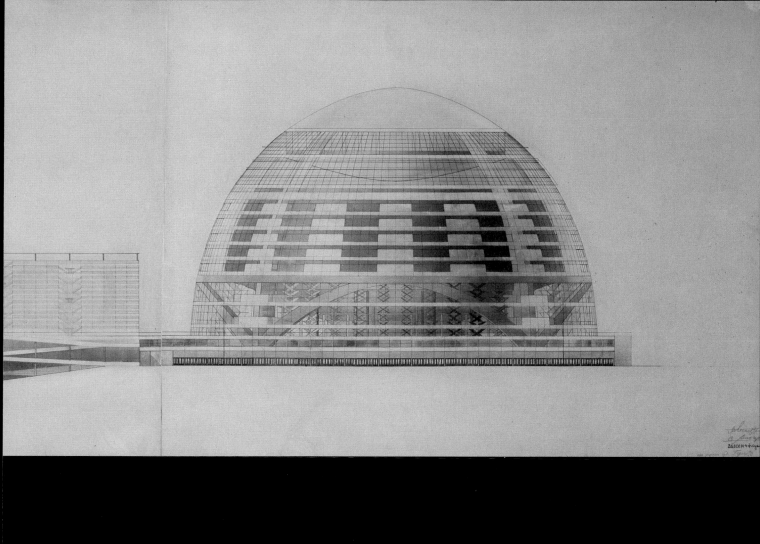

Opposite:
102 Nikolai Ladovsky
Palace of Soviets
Competition project, first (preliminary) stage
unexecuted
Moscow, February–May 1931
Facade
Ink on paper
25⅞ × 37⅜″ (65.8 × 95 cm)

103 Nikolai Ladovsky
Palace of Soviets
Competition project, first (preliminary) stage
unexecuted
Moscow, February–May 1931
Facade
Ink on paper
24⅝ × 36⅝″ (62.5 × 93 cm)

Opposite:
105 Alexander, Leonid, and Viktor Vesnin
Palace of Soviets
Competition project, fourth stage, second
version
Moscow, August 1932–February 1933
Perspective
Colored pencil, pencil, watercolor, white ink,
ink, and collage on paper
30¼ × 50⅜" (77 × 128 cm)
Drawing executed by Vladimir and Georgi
Stenberg

106 Vladimir Gelfreikh and Vladimir Shchuko
Palace of Soviets
Competition project, fourth stage, unexecuted
Moscow, August 1932–February 1933
Perspective
Pencil, ink, gouache, watercolor, white ink,
and collage on paper
21¾ × 39″ (55 × 99 cm)

107 Ivan Zholtovsky
Palace of Soviets
Competition project, second (open) stage,
unexecuted
Awarded one of three "first prizes"
Moscow, July–December 1931
Perspective
Sanguine on paper
14 × 22⅞″ (35.5 × 58 cm)

Opposite:
108 Vladimir Gelfreikh, Boris Iofan, Vladimir
Shchuko, and Sergei Merkurov (sculptor)
Palace of Soviets
Commissioned amended project, in response to
the Jury Statement of 10 May 1933, unexecuted
Moscow, probably May–August 1933
Perspective
Ink and applied color on paper
48½ × 37¾″ (123 × 96 cm)

110 Alexander, Leonid, and Viktor Vesnin
Commissariat of Heavy Industry,
Narkomtiazhprom
Competition project, first version, unexecuted
Moscow, 1934
Perspective
Ink, watercolor, pencil, and white ink on paper
17¼ × 43½″ (44 × 110.5 cm)

111 Alexander, Leonid, and Viktor Vesnin
Commissariat of Heavy Industry,
Narkomtiazhprom
Competition project, first version, unexecuted
Moscow, 1934
Perspective
Ink, gouache, and pencil on tracing paper
8 × 12½″ (20 × 32 cm)

Opposite:
112 Konstantin Melnikov, with participation of V. M. Lebedev, Nikolai Trankvilitsky, and Nikolai Khryakov
Commissariat of Heavy Industry, Narkomtiazhprom
Moscow, 1934
Perspective
Ink on paper
57½ × 77″ (146 × 195.5 cm)

113 Konstantin Melnikov, with participation of V. M. Lebedev, Nikolai Trankvilitsky, and Nikolai Khryakov
Commissariat of Heavy Industry, Narkomtiazhprom
Competition project, unexecuted
Moscow, 1934
Site plan
Ink and colored ink on paper
29⅜ × 31⅛″ (74.5 × 79 cm)

114 Konstantin Melnikov, with participation
of V. M. Lebedev, Nikolai Trankvilitsky, and
Nikolai Khryakov
*Commissariat of Heavy Industry,
Narkomtiazhprom*
Unexecuted
Moscow, 1934
North elevation
Ink on paper
31¾ × 35½″ (80.5 × 90 cm)

115 Konstantin Melnikov, with participation
of V. M. Lebedev, Nikolai Trankvilitsky, and
Nikolai Khryakov
*Commissariat of Heavy Industry,
Narkomtiazhprom*
Competition project, unexecuted
Moscow, 1934
Elevation to Red Square
Ink and watercolor on paper
28⅜ × 45¼″ (72 × 115 cm)

Opposite:
116 Konstantin Melnikov, with participation
of V. M. Lebedev, Nikolai Trankvilitsky, and
Nikolai Khryakov
*Commissariat of Heavy Industry,
Narkomtiazhprom*
Unexecuted
Moscow, 1934
Perspective view into one of two entrances
from Red Square
Ink and watercolor on paper
58¼ × 59½″ (148 × 151 cm)

117 Ivan Leonidov
*Commissariat of Heavy Industry,
Narkomtiazhprom*
Competition project, unexecuted
Moscow, 1934
Elevational view from northwest corner of Red
Square, with round tower visible between the
other two
Ink, watercolor, and white ink on paper
25⅝ × 54″ (65 × 137 cm)

118 Ivan Leonidov
*Commissariat of Heavy Industry,
Narkomtiazhprom*
Competition project, unexecuted
Moscow, 1934
Elevation to Red Square
Ink, watercolor, white ink, and bronze
powder on paper
32¼ × 55½″ (82 × 141 cm)

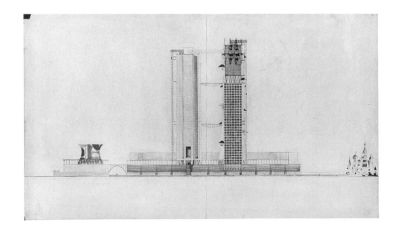

Opposite:
119 Ivan Leonidov
*Commissariat of Heavy Industry,
Narkomtiazhprom*
Competition project, unexecuted
Moscow, 1934
Perspective looking north along Red Square
elevation toward Bolshoi Theater
Ink and watercolor on paper
69⅞ × 46½″ (177.5 × 117.5 cm)

120 Ivan Leonidov
Commissariat of Heavy Industry,
Narkomtiazhprom
Competition project, unexecuted
Moscow, 1934
Perspective sketch through cupolas of
St. Basil's Cathedral
Ink on paper on plywood
19¾ × 19¾″ (50 × 50 cm)

121 Ivan Leonidov
Commissariat of Heavy Industry,
Narkomtiazhprom
Competition project, unexecuted
Moscow, 1934
Perspective sketch with a view of the
Kremlin
Paper and ink on plywood
19¾ × 19¾″ (50 × 50 cm)

122 Ivan Leonidov
*Commissariat of Heavy Industry,
Narkomtiazhprom*
Competition project, unexecuted
Moscow, 1934
Perspective through the main entrance arch
looking out across Red Square to the Lenin
Mausoleum
Pastel on paper
22½ × 14½″ (57 × 37 cm)

123 Ivan Leonidov
*Commissariat of Heavy Industry,
Narkomtiazhprom*
Competition project, unexecuted
Moscow, 1934
General plan
Ink, gouache, and white ink on doubled
tracing paper
17¾ × 40⅛″ (45 × 102 cm)

124 Ivan Leonidov
Commissariat of Heavy Industry,
Narkomtiazhprom
Competition project, unexecuted
Moscow, 1934
Perspective detail looking up the rectangular
tower
Ink, gouache, and white ink on paper
63¾ × 17¾" (162 × 45 cm)

Following the closing of the National Academy of Architecture, the Museum of Architecture and the A. V. Shchusev State Museum of Russian Architecture were united. Today the museum's resources total approximately 700,000 objects, including about 200,000 examples of architectural graphic art, thousands of decorative-applied artworks, unusual furniture, and more than 500,000 photographs and negatives of architectural monuments and modern buildings.

The workshop-studios of prominent architects such as Shchusev, Melnikov, Zholtovsky, and the Vesnin brothers have or will become affiliate branches of the museum. In cooperation with the Academy of Sciences of the USSR, another of these branch museums is currently being organized to display the work of the noted Russian engineer V. G. Shukov (1853–1939), who designed many unique architectural constructions. His famous radio tower on Shabolovka Street in Moscow will be included in this museum, along with his industrial constructions built in other Soviet cities. These will be dismantled and relocated to the museum for exhibition. Yet another goal for future affiliate museums is the reconstruction of groups of architectural ensembles from different regions of the USSR.

Of particular note among the museum's resources is the collection of projects of the Soviet avant-garde of the 1920s and '30s. More than five hundred architectural competitions were held in the USSR during that period, and materials from the most prestigious of these competitions form the core of this collection. Beginning with the Palace of Labor competition in Moscow, they became veritable proving grounds for original concepts and ideas that fostered new creative directions in Soviet architecture. The ideas put forward by many of these architects influenced their colleagues within the Soviet Union as well as architects throughout the world.

Competitions were the meeting places at which the new came face to face with the old, where new types of buildings were formulated, such as "people's houses" and workers' clubs. A search for the prototypical "socialist" architectural form was accomplished by means of projects for the Palace of Labor (1922–23), the Palace of Soviets of the USSR (1931–33), and the People's Commissariat of Heavy Industry (1934–35).

In 1935 the museum acquired the first papers in this collection of Soviet avant-garde materials: the projects for the Palace of Soviets competition, as well as materials relating to other important projects, notably the competition projects for the V. I. Lenin Library and for the V. I. Nemirovich-Danchenko Music Theater. In 1939 the museum acquired all of the competition projects for the People's Commissariat of Heavy Industry.

Important additions to the museum during the 1960s and '70s were the creative archives of major architects such as Shchusev, the Vesnin brothers, M. V. Ginzburg, Zholtovsky, Fomin, V. F. Krinsky, and B. M. Iofan, which were donated either by the architects or their families. I. I. Leonidov's projects for the Palace of Culture were given to the museum by the architect N. B. Sokolov, who also donated his own project for a health-resort hotel, which he had completed in 1928 as a course assignment while a student at the VKhUTEMAS. The Moscow Architectural Institute donated additional drawings by Krinsky, a gift that significantly augmented the museum's existing material relating to his work. As a result of these many contributions, the Shchusev Museum has become the central repository of original materials documenting the history of Soviet architecture.

I. A. Kazus
Acting Director
A. V. Shchusev State Research Museum of Architecture

Translated from the Russian by Andrew Stivelman

Biographies of the Architects

Grigori Borisovich Barkhin

Born 1880 in Perm'; died 1969 in Moscow

1901—08
Studied at the Architecture School of the Academy of Arts in St. Petersburg under Pomerantsev

1909—14
Assistant to R. Klein (Yusupov Tomb in Arkhangelsk; interiors of the Pushkin Museum of Fine Arts; Borodinsky Bridge in Moscow)

From 1909
Taught in Moscow

1928—30
Editor-in-chief of the *Annuals of the Moscow Architectural Society* (MAO)

Main works to 1935:

1924—26
Competition projects for a people's home and a spinning mill for Ivanovo-Voznesensk (with M. Barkhin)

1926—27
Built the headquarters for the newspaper *Izvestiia* in Moscow (with M. Barkhin)

1928—29
Built a sanatorium in Saki, Crimea (with M. Barkhin)

1930—32
Competition projects for theaters in Rostov-on-the-Don and Sverdlovsk; extensive town-planning work

Mikhail Grigorievich Barkhin

Born 1906 in Bobruisk, son of Grigori Barkhin; died 1986 in Moscow

1922—24
Studied at the Moscow Institute of Civil Engineering under P. Golosov and L. Vesnin

From 1930
Taught at the Moscow Architectural Institute

Main works to 1935:

1924—29
Joint projects in Ivanovo-Voznesensk and Saki (with his father, G. Barkhin)

1926—27
Built the headquarters building for the newspaper *Izvestiia* in Moscow (with G. Barkhin)

1929
Training center of the automobile factory in Gorky (prize-winning competition project with G. Barkhin, partially executed)

1930—33
Project for V. Meyerhold Theater in Moscow (with S. Vakhtangov)

Andrei Evgenievich Belogrud

Born 1875 in Zhitomir; died 1933 in Gatchina (near Leningrad)

1901—10
Studied at the Architecture School of the Academy of Arts in St. Petersburg under L. Benois

1919—22
Rector of the Free Artistic Studios (Svomas) in Petrograd (from 1921, the Academy of Arts)

Main works:

1913—19
Built the Rozenshtein house and other apartment buildings in Petrograd

1919
Competition project for a Workers' Palace in Petrograd

1923
Competition project for the Palace of Labor in Moscow

1924
Competition project for the Anglo-Russian Trading Company (ARCOS) building in Moscow

1925
Competition project for the Lenin House of the People, Ivanovo-Voznesensk

Iakov Georgievich Chernikhov

Born 1899 in Pavlograd (now Dnepropetrovsk region); died 1951 in Moscow

1917
Completed higher pedagogical courses at the Academy of Arts in Petrograd

1925
Graduated from the Architecture School of the Academy. Taught drawing at the Leningrad Institute of Railway Engineers

Main works to 1935:

Throughout the 1920s
Architectural fantasies and other graphic work, published in his books *Fundamentals of Contemporary Architecture* (1930 and 1931), *Construction of Architectural and Machine Forms* (1931), and *Architectural Fantasies: 101 Compositions* (1933)

Late 1920s
Chemical factories and metallurgical plants in Kiev, Leningrad, Kutaisi, Dnepropetrovsk, Minsk, Novosibirsk, and other cities

1931—32
Department store in Leningrad; chemical plants in Novosibirsk and other cities

Vladimir Ivanovich Fidman

Born 1884; died 1949

1910
Graduated from the Architecture School of the Academy of Arts in St. Petersburg

1918
Studied further under I. Zholtovsky at the VKhUTEMAS in Moscow

1919
Member of Zhivskulptarkh

1921
Member of Inkhuk

1923
Member of the Association of New Architects (ASNOVA)

Main works to 1935:

1919
Competition project for the Moscow Crematorium (with Krinsky)

1925
Competition projects for the Institute of Mineral Raw Materials, Moscow (alone), and for the Republican Hospital in Samarkand (with Fridman)

1928
Competition project for the Lenin Library in Moscow (with Markov and Fridman)

1931
Competition project for the Palace of Soviets, Moscow

Ivan Alexandrovich Fomin

Born 1872 in Orel; died 1936 in Moscow

1894—97 and 1905—09
Studied at the Architecture School of the Academy of Arts in St. Petersburg under L. Benois and V. Mate

1900
Assistant to Kekushev and Shekhtel in Moscow; contributor to the journal *Mir Iskusstva* (The World of Art)

1919
Headed the first Soviet Architectural and Planning Studio for the city of Petrograd

Main works:

1911—14
Built the Polovtsev and Abamelek-Lazarev Houses; New Petersburg development et al in St. Petersburg

1919
Competition projects for the Workers' Palace and Crematorium in Petrograd

1924
Competition projects for the Soviet pavilion at the 1925 Exposition des Arts Décoratifs in Paris and the Sverdlov monument in Moscow

1928—31
Built the Dynamo company building and extension to the Mossoviet (Moscow Council) complex in Moscow; project for the building for the People's Commissariat of Transport and Communications in Moscow

1934
Competition project for Narkomtiazhprom building, Red Square, in Moscow

Daniil Fedorovich Fridman

Born 1887 in Odessa; died 1950 in Moscow

1908—15
Studied at the Moscow School of Painting, Sculpture and Architecture

1927—32
Taught at the VKhUTEMAS and the Moscow Architectural Institute

1928
Member of the Union of Architects and Urbanists (ARU)

Main works to 1935:

1911–12
Built several private houses in Moscow

1913–19
Projects for commercial buildings in Moscow, Nizhnyi Novgorod, and Orenburg

1921–22
Built a workers' housing district in Tashkent

1923
Competition project for the Anglo-Russian Trading Company (ARCOS) building in Moscow (with Eikhenvald)

1925
Competition project for the Republican Hospital in Samarkand (with Fidman)

1928
Competition project for the Lenin Library in Moscow (with Markov and Fidman)

1931
Competition project for the replanning of Moscow; project for Trubnaia Square in Moscow (in an ARU team)

Alexander Ivanovich Gegello

Born 1891 in Ekaterinoslav (now Dneprpetrovsk); died 1965 in Moscow

1911–20
Studied architecture at the Institute of Civil Engineers in St. Petersburg/Petrograd

1918–22
Studied at the Painting School of the Academy of Arts in Petrograd under Bilibin et al

1915–18
During studies worked as an architectural assistant to Fomin

1924–31
Taught at the Second Polytechnical Institute and the Institute of Communal Construction in Leningrad

Main works to 1935:

1923
Projects for low-rise workers' housing in Leningrad

1924
Competition project for the Anglo-Russian Trading Company (ARCOS) building in Moscow

1925–27
Built the Tractor Street housing district (with Nikolsky, Simonov, and Krichevsky) and the Moscow-Narva district House of Culture (with Krichevsky), both in Leningrad

1927–29
Built extensions to the Botkin Hospital, Leningrad (with Krichevsky)

Vladimir Georgievich Gelfreikh

Born 1885 in Petersburg; died 1967 in Moscow

1906–14
Studied at the Architecture School of the Academy of Arts in St. Petersburg under L. Benois

Main works to 1935 (all with V. Shchuko):

1923–25
Built the Propylae (gatehouses) at the Smolny Institute in Leningrad

1925
Built the Monument to Lenin at the Finland Station in Leningrad

1928–52
Built the Lenin Library in Moscow

1932
Competition projects for the Palace of Soviets in Moscow, and from 1933, assistant to B. Iofan on the final project designs

Moisei Iakovlevich Ginzburg

Born 1892 in Minsk; died 1946 in Moscow

1914
Graduated from the Academy of Fine Arts in Milan

1914–17
Studied in the Architectural Division of the Riga Polytechnical Institute in Moscow

From 1922
Taught in the Architectural Faculty at the Moscow Higher Technical College (MVTU)

1924
Published *Style and Epoch*

1925–26
One of the founders of the Constructivist architectural group, the Union of Contemporary Architects (OSA), and an editor of their journal, *Sovremennaia arkhitektura* (Contemporary Architecture)

1932
Elected to the Board of the Union of Soviet Architects

Main works to 1935:

1922–27
Numerous competition projects, including the Palace of Labor, Orgametal building, and the House of Textiles in Moscow

1928–30
Built the experimental housing complex for the People's Commissariat of Finance, Narkomfin, in Moscow (with I. Milinis)

1928–31
Competition project for the government building in Alma-Ata (with I. Milinis) (executed)

1931–32
Competition projects for the Palace of Soviets in Moscow (with S. Lisagor and G. Gassenpflug)

1933
Competition project for the Nemirovich-Danchenko Theater in Moscow (with G. Gassenpflug)

1934
Competition project for the Narkomtiazhprom building, Red Square, in Moscow

Ilia Alexandrovich Golosov

Born 1883 in Moscow; died 1945 in
Moscow

1912
Graduated from the Moscow School of
Painting, Sculpture and Architecture

From 1919
Taught at the Moscow Higher Technical
College (MVTU), then at the VKhUTEMAS
and at the Moscow Architectural Institute

Member of the Union of Contemporary
Architects (OSA)

Main works to 1935:

1923
Competition project for the Palace of Labor
in Moscow; built Far Eastern Pavilion at
the All-Russian Agricultural and Handicraft Industries Exhibition in Moscow

1924
Competition projects for the Soviet pavilion at the Exposition des Arts Décoratifs
in Paris, 1925; the *Leningrad Pravda* building in Moscow; the Lenin House of the
People in Ivanovo-Voznesensk

1926
Zuev Workers' Club in Moscow (executed);
competition projects for the Central Telegraph and Electrobank buildings in
Moscow

1928
Project for communal housing in
Stalingrad

1932
Competition project for the Palace of Soviets in Moscow

Panteleimon Alexandrovich Golosov

Born 1882 in Moscow; died 1945 in
Moscow

1911
Graduated from the Moscow School of
Painting, Sculpture and Architecture

From 1918
Taught at the State Free Artistic Studios
(Svomas) and subsequently at the
VKhUTEMAS and the Moscow Architec-
tural Institute

Member of the Union of Contemporary
Architects (OSA)

Main works to 1935:

1919
Worked under Shchusev and Zholtovsky on
Moscow city planning

1923
Series of pavilions for the All-Russian
Agricultural and Handicraft Industries
Exhibition in Moscow

1930–34
Built the headquarters and printing works
of the newspaper *Pravda* in Moscow

Georgi Pavlovich Golts

Born 1893 in Bolshevo near Moscow;
died 1946 in Moscow

1913–15
Studied at the Moscow School of Painting,
Sculpture and Architecture

1919
After war service resumed study, in the
VKhUTEMAS under Ladovsky

1922
Graduation project won him a trip to Italy

From 1926
Member of the Moscow Architectural
Society (MAO)

Main works to 1935:

1923
Participated in the design and construc-
tion of the All-Russian Agricultural and
Handicraft Industries Exhibition in
Moscow

1927–35
Worked in collaboration with Zholtovsky,
particularly on industrial projects

1930
Competition project for the Palace of Cul-
ture of the Proletarsky district in Moscow
(MAO team with Parusnikov and Sobolev)

1931
Competition project for the Palace of
Soviets in Moscow

1934
Project for reconstruction of the Kamernyi
Theater in Moscow

Boris Mikhailovich Iofan

Born 1891 in Odessa; died 1976 in
Moscow

1903–11
Studied painting and sculpture at the
Odessa Arts School

1914–19
Studied architecture at the Higher Institute of Fine Arts and at the Higher School
of Engineering in Rome; was an assistant
to the architect Brazini

Main works to 1935:

1916–22
Built several private houses in the suburbs
of Rome; Ambroggia Chapel at the San
Lorenzo Cemetery in Rome

1925
Competition project for workers' housing
on Rusakovskaia Street in Moscow
(executed)

1928–31
Built housing and amenities complex for
Communist Party officials on Serafimovich
Street in Moscow (with D. M. Iofan)

1931–33
Winning entry in the Palace of Soviets
competition in Moscow, progressed to
working drawings with Shchuko, Gelfreikh
et al thereafter (begun, not completed)

Alexander Iakovlevich Karra

Born 1904; died 1944

Member of the Association of New Architects (ASNOVA) and, after its formation in
1929, of the Proletarian Architects' Organization (VOPRA)

Main works to 1935:

1931
Competition projects for the first stage of
the Palace of Soviets in Moscow (as part of
the team of VOPRA architects under
Alabian) and for the second stage
independently

1932
Competition project for a Palace of Labor
in Moscow (with Lamtsov and Egorychev)

Nikolai Iakovlevich Kolli

Born 1894 in Moscow; died 1966 in Moscow

1922
Graduated from the VKhUTEMAS in Moscow

Main works to 1935:

1918
Participated in the decoration of Moscow for the first anniversary of the Revolution, designing a symbolic construction, *The Red Wedge*, for Revolution Square

1923
Worked on pavilions for the All-Russian Agricultural and Handicraft Industries Exhibition in Moscow

1927—32
Participated in the planning for the Dneproges (Dnepr Hydroelectric Station), under the direction of V. Vesnin

1928—36
As executive architect in Moscow for the construction of Le Corbusier's Tsentrosoyuz building, worked in his Paris office, 1928—29, and supervised the project until completion

Lidia Konstantinovna Komarova

Born 1902 in Ivanovo-Voznesensk

1922—29
Studied at the VKhUTEMAS under N. Ladovsky and later A. Vesnin

1929—30
Member of the editorial board of the journal, *Sovremennaia arkhitektura* (Contemporary Architecture)

Member of the Union of Contemporary Architects (OSA)

Main works to 1935:

1929
Graduation project for the Comintern building in Moscow

1931
Competition project for the Palace of Soviets in Moscow (with I. Vainshtein and Iu. Mushinksy)

1932
Competition project with other Constructivists for a cultural, residential, and sports complex, Krasnaia Presnia district, in Moscow

Vladimir Fedorovich Krinsky

Born 1890 in Riazan; died 1971 in Moscow

1910—17
Studied at the Architecture School of the Academy of Arts in St. Petersburg

1919
Member of the Zhivskulptarkh group

1920—30
Taught at the VKhUTEMAS (one of the directors of the basic course)

From 1921
Member of the Institute of Artistic Culture (Inkhuk) in Moscow

From 1930
Taught at the Moscow Architectural Institute

One of the founders of the Association of New Architects (ASNOVA)

Main works to 1935:

1919
Competition project for a crematorium in Moscow (with Fidman)

1920—23
Experimental research projects: "Color and Form," "Color and Spatial Composition," "Color and Graphic Composition"; skyscraper project for Vesenkha headquarters on Lubianskaia Square (now Dzerzhinsky Square) in Moscow

1923—24
Competition projects for the Palace of Labor and the building for the Anglo-Russian Trading Company (ARCOS) in Moscow; project for the Lenin House of the People in Ivanovo-Voznesensk; the Lenin Mausoleum

1931
Project for the Palace of Soviets in Moscow

Georgi Tikhonovich Krutikov

Born 1899 in Voronezh; died 1958 in Moscow

1922—28
Studied at the VKhUTEMAS

Member of the Association of New Architects (ASNOVA) and the Association of Architects and Urbanists (ARU)

Main works to 1935:

1928
Graduation project for a "Flying City"

1929—30
Competition project for a Palace of Culture in the Proletarsky district in Moscow (in an ARU team)

1930
Competition project for a socialist city and for the Avtostroi automobile building combine in Nizhnyi Novogorod (with Lavrov and Popov)

1931
Competition project for the Palace of Soviets in Moscow (in an ARU team)

1933—39
Competition project for the Nemirovich-Danchenko Music Theater in Moscow (partially executed)

Nikolai Alexandrovich Ladovsky

Born 1881 in Moscow; died 1941 in Moscow

1914—17
Studied at the Moscow School of Painting, Sculpture and Architecture

1919
Member of the Zhivskulptarkh group

From 1920
Taught at the VKhUTEMAS (one of the directors of the basic course)

From 1921
Member of the Institute of Artistic Culture (Inkhuk) in Moscow

1923
Principal theorist of the Rationalist approach and one of the founders of the Association of New Architects (ASNOVA). Editor, with El Lissitzky, of their journal, *Izvestiia ASNOVA* (ASNOVA News), 1926

1928
Founder of the Union of Architects and Urbanists (ARU)

1932
Elected to the Board of the Union of Soviet Architects

Main works to 1935:

1919–20
Experimental projects of dynamic compositions

1929–30
Project for the layout of a labor commune in the settlement of Kostino; "Parabola" project for the reconstruction of Moscow; competition project for the "Green City" near Moscow

1931
Competition projects for the Palace of Soviets in Moscow

Ivan Vasilevich Lamtsov

Born 1899 in Filippovichi (now Riazan region)

1916–18
Studied at the Moscow School of Painting, Sculpture and Architecture

1926
Graduated from the VKhUTEMAS; continued as a teacher there and later at the Moscow Architectural Institute

Member of the Association of New Architects (ASNOVA)

Main works of the 1920s:

1921–23
VKhUTEMAS assignments on the manifestations of dynamics, rhythm, relationships, and proportions (under N. Ladovsky)

1923
Contributed to the All-Russian Agricultural and Handicraft Industries Exhibition in Moscow

1924
Red Stadium project in the Vorobev Mountains in Moscow (part of a team of VKhUTEMAS students); awarded a Grand Prix at the Exposition des Arts Décoratifs in Paris, 1925

1926
Sports club Krasnye Khamovniki in Moscow (project with V. Petrov; partially executed)

Ivan Ilich Leonidov

Born 1902 in Babino (now Kalinin region); died 1959 in Moscow

1921–27
Studied at the VKhUTEMAS under A. Vesnin and continued to teach there until 1930. Member of the Union of Contemporary Architects (ISA) and the editorial board of the journal *Sovremennaia arkhitektura* (Contemporary Architecture)

Main works to 1935:

1926
Student project for the headquarters and printing works of the newspaper *Izvestiia* in Moscow

1927
Graduation project for the Lenin Institute of Librarianship in the Lenin Hills in Moscow

1928
Experimental project for a Workers' Club of New Social Type

1928–29
Competition projects for a film factory, industrial headquarters building, and the Tsentrosoyuz building in Moscow

1930
Competition projects for the Palace of Culture of the Proletarsky district of Moscow, and for the workers' settlement at the Magnitogorsk industrial combine

1934
Competition project for the Narkomtiazhprom building, Red Square, in Moscow

Konstantin Stepanovich Melnikov

Born 1890 in Moscow; died 1976 in Moscow

1905–17
Studied at the Moscow School of Painting, Sculpture and Architecture

1918–20
Worked in the planning studio of the Moscow Council (Mossoviet) under Zholtovsky and Shchusev

1921–23
Taught at the VKhUTEMAS

Main works to 1935:

1922
Competition projects for workers' housing and for the Palace of Labor in Moscow

1923
Built the Makhorka Pavilion for the All-Russian Agricultural and Handicraft Industries Exhibition in Moscow

1924–25
Competition projects for the Moscow bureau of the newspaper *Leningrad Pravda*; for the USSR Pavilion of the Exposition des Arts Décoratifs in Paris, 1925 (executed)

1927–31
Built the Rusakov Club, the Kauchuk (Rubber) Factory Club, the Gorky Palace of Culture, the Burevesnik Factory Club in Moscow, three bus garages, and his own private house in Moscow

1932
Competition project for the Palace of Soviets in Moscow (ignored by jury)

1934
Competition project for the Narkomtiazhprom building, Red Square, in Moscow

Mikhail Adolfovich Minkus

Born 1905 in Odessa; died 1963 in Turku (Finland)

1923–25
Studied in the Architecture Faculty of the Odessa Arts School while working as assistant to his father, A. Minkus

1925–30
Studied in the Architecture School of the Academy of Arts, Leningrad, also working for Fomin and Shchuko

From 1930
Worked in Moscow

Member of Moscow Architectural Society (MAO)

Main works to 1935:

1923
Competition project for the Palace of Labor in Moscow (with A. Minkus)

1924
Competition project for the Anglo-Russian Trading Company (ARCOS) building in Moscow (with A. Minkus)

1926
Competition project for the House of Textiles in Moscow (with A. Minkus)

1928
Pre-graduation project for a bus garage

1928–29
Built the Kiev state shoe factory (with A. Minkus)

1931
Various projects for bus and car garages

1934
Competition project for the Narkomtiazhprom building, Red Square, in Moscow (in Fomin's team)

Mikhail Ivanovich Motylev

Born 1891 in Moscow; died 1969

1916
Graduated from the Moscow School of Painting, Sculpture and Architecture

1919
Graduated from the Painting School of the Academy of Arts in Petrograd. Worked in the architectural offices of Pomerantsev and Shchusev

From 1934
Taught in the Moscow Architectural Institute

Main works to 1935:

1926–27
Built workers' housing complexes on Rusakovskaia, Dubrovskaia, Boevskaia, Novo-Riazanskaia streets and other sites in Moscow (in a municipal design team)

1929
Built a communal housing development on Liusinovskaia Street in Moscow

1929–33
Built the Bolshaia Dangerovka housing district in Moscow (in a design team)

Leonid Nikolaevich Pavlov

Born 1909 in Manglis, Georgia

1930
Graduated from the VKhUTEMAS, where he studied under V. Vesnin and Leonidov; continued to teach there through change to Moscow Architectural Institute in 1934

Student member of the Constructivist architects' group, OSA (from May 1930: SASS)

Main works to 1935:

1929–30
Project for an intercollegiate design competition for a student housing commune in Leningrad; student project done in Leonidov's studio (with N. Pavlov)

1929–31
Series of projects for rebuilding Moscow squares (in an OSA–SASS team)

1931
Competition projects for the Palace of Soviets in Moscow (member of two SASS teams)

Vladimir Alexeevich Shchuko

Born 1878 in Berlin; died 1939 in Moscow

1896–1904
Studied in the Architecture School of the Academy of Arts in St. Petersburg

1905–07
Traveled to Turkey, Greece, and Italy. Took part in exhibitions of The World of Art group

1908–11
Set designer at the Old Theater in St. Petersburg

1911
Architect of the Russian pavilions at international exhibitions in Paris and Rome. Made Academician

Main works to 1935:

1914
Built the Memorial Hall at the Academy of Arts in Petrograd

1917–20
Participated in mass-propaganda work, including a Monument to Heroes of the Revolution in Helsinki and the decoration of Petrograd during the festivals commemorating the Revolution

1918
Active member of the Architectural Subsection of IZO, the arts administration of the Commissariat of Enlightenment

From 1919
Director of the architecture studio at the State Free Studios (Svomas) in Petrograd

1923
Built the Foreign Section Pavilions at the All-Russian Agricultural and Handicraft Industries Exhibition in Moscow

1926
Built the monument to Lenin at the Finland Station in Leningrad (with Gelfreikh)

1928
First project for the Lenin State Library of the USSR in Moscow (with Gelfreikh; executed)

1932
Competition projects for the Palace of Soviets in Moscow (with Gelfreikh). From 1933, deputy project director to B. Iofan on the final designs

Alexei Viktorovich Shchusev

Born 1873 in Kishinev; died 1949 in Moscow

1891—97
Studied in the Architecture School of the Academy of Arts in St. Petersburg

1920
Taught at the VKhUTEMAS

From 1921
President of the Moscow Architectural Society (MAO)

1926—29
Director of the State Tretyakov Gallery

Main works to 1935:

1908—12
Church restoration projects; Marfo-Marinsky Church in Moscow and private houses built

1911
Design for the Kazan Station in Moscow (building continued until 1941)

1913—14
Russian Pavilion at the international exhibition in Venice

1923
With Zholtovsky planned and supervised the All-Russian Agricultural and Handicraft Industries Exhibition in Moscow

1924
First temporary mausoleum for Lenin on Red Square in Moscow

1925
Competition project for the Central Telegraph building in Moscow

1926—30
Final design and building of the Lenin Mausoleum

1927—28
Built the Novaia Matsesta sanatorium in Sochi

1928—33
Built the Agricultural Commissariat headquarters, Narkomzen, in Moscow

1929—30
Project for the Government Center in Samarkand

1931—33
Competition projects for the Palace of Soviets in Moscow

Nikolai Borisovich Sokolov

Born 1904 in St. Petersburg

1925—30
Studied at the VKhUTEMAS, latterly under A. Vesnin

Member of the Constructivists' architectural group, OSA

Main works to 1935:

1928
Student project for a health-resort hotel

1930
Competition project for workers' settlement at the Magnitogorsk industrial combine (in an OSA team)

1931—32
Project for the planning of Chardzhui (in a team)

The Vesnin Brothers

Alexander Alexandrovich Vesnin

Born 1883 in Yurevets; died 1959 in Moscow

1907—11
Studied painting in the studios of Tsionglinsky and Yuon

1903—12
Studied architecture at the Institute of Civil Engineering in St. Petersburg

1911
First exhibited as a painter

1912—13
Shared a studio with V. Tatlin in Moscow

1918
Decorated Red Square for May 1 festivities (with V. Vesnin)

1919—20
Set designer for the Maly Theater in Moscow

From 1921
Member of the Institute of Artistic Culture (Inkhuk) in Moscow

1921
Participated in the "5 × 5 = 25" exhibition of Constructivist artists

1921—23
Set designer for the Kamernyi (Chamber) Theater in Moscow, including pioneering Constructivist designs such as those for G. K. Chesterton's *The Man Who Was Thursday,* exhibited at the Exposition des Arts Décoratifs, Paris, 1925, winning "honorable mention"

1921—25
Taught at the VKhUTEMAS in Moscow

From 1925
Co-chairman with M. Ginzburg of the Constructivist architects' group, the Union of Contemporary Architects (OSA); from 1926, co-editor with Ginzburg of their journal, *Sovremennaia arkhitektura* (Contemporary Architecture)

Leonid Alexandrovich Vesnin

Born 1880 in Yurevets; died 1933 in Moscow

1900—09
Studied in the Architecture School of the Academy of Arts in St. Petersburg under L. Benois

From 1923
Professor at the Moscow Higher Technical College (MVTU)

From 1925
Member of the Union of Contemporary Architects (OSA)

Main individual works:

1918—19
Shatursk electric power station and related housing

1921—22
Design and construction of a series of workers' settlements

Viktor Alexandrovich Vesnin

Born 1882 in Yurevets; died 1933 in Moscow

1901–12
Studied architecture at the Institute of Civil Engineering in St. Petersburg

1906–09
Worked in the Moscow architectural offices of Ivanov-Shits and R. Klein

1913–14
Spent in Italy

1918
Decorated Red Square for May 1 celebration (with A. Vesnin)

From 1923
Professor at both the Moscow Higher Technical College (MVTU) and the VKhUTEMAS

From 1925
Member of the Union of Contemporary Architects (OSA)

1932
Elected to the Board of the Union of Soviet Architects

Main individual works to 1935:

1915
Built chemical plants in Tambov province and near Kineshma

1918–19
Built the Chernorechensky super-phosphate factory in Rastiapik and a chemical factory in Saratov

1925
Built the Institute of Mineral Raw Materials in Moscow

1926–27
Built the Agricultural Bank building, Ivselbank, in Ivanovo-Voznesensk

Main Architectural Works Done by A., L., and V. Vesnin Together, to 1935:

1910–13
In the offices of older architects, built various commercial and banking buildings in Moscow; facade of the Central Post Office

1914
Built a house for D. Sorotkin, Nizhnyi Novgorod

1923
Competition project for the Palace of Labor in Moscow

1924
Competition projects for the Moscow bureau of the newspaper *Leningrad Pravda* (A. and V. Vesnin only) and the Anglo-Russian Trading Company (ARCOS) building in Moscow

1927
Built the Mostorg department store, Krasnaia Presnia, in Moscow (A. and L. Vesnin only)

1928–29
A series of commissioned projects for the Lenin Library in Moscow

1931–37
Commissioned design, partly executed, for the Palace of Culture of the Proletarsky district in Moscow

1932–33
Competition projects for the Palace of Soviets in Moscow

1934
Competition projects for the Narkom-tiazhprom building, Red Square, in Moscow

Ivan Vladislavovich Zholtovsky

Born 1867 in Pinsk (near Brest); died 1959 in Moscow

1887–98
Studied in the Architecture School of the Academy of Arts in St. Petersburg

From 1900
Member of Moscow Architectural Society (MAO)

1900–32
Taught in the Stroganov Arts and Crafts School, continuing when it became part of the VKhUTEMAS

1932
Elected to the Board of the Union of Soviet Architects

Main works to 1935:

1903–05
Built the clubhouse of the Horse Racing Club, Moscow

1909–10
Built the mansion of G. Tarasov in Moscow

1911–12
Built a textile factory in Kostroma region

1923
With Shchusev, planned and supervised the All-Russian Agricultural and Handicraft Industries Exhibition in Moscow; built several pavilions

1925–26
Built the Soviet pavilion at the Milan international exhibition, visiting Italy

1927–28
Built the generator building of the Moscow Central Power Station (MOGES)

1931–33
Competition projects for the Palace of Soviets in Moscow

1933–34
Built the apartment building "on the Mokhovaia" in Moscow

Selected Bibliography

Compiled by Catherine Cooke

General Studies of Arts and Culture of the Period

Elliott, David. *New Worlds: Russian Art and Society 1900–1937*. New York: Rizzoli, 1986.

Fauchereau, Serge, ed. *Moscow 1900–1930: Collected Essays*. New York: Rizzoli, 1988.

Fülöp-Miller, René. *The Mind and Face of Bolshevism: An Examination of Cultural Life in Soviet Russia*. London and New York: G. P. Putnam, 1927, republished New York, 1962.

Bibliographies (Materials in Russian and Western Languages)

Senkevitch, Anatole. *Soviet Architecture 1917–1962: A Bibliographical Guide to Source Material*. Charlottesville: University Press of Virginia, 1974.

Starr, S. Frederick. "Writings of the 1960s on the Modern Movement in Russia." *Journal of the Society of Architectural Historians* (Summer 1971): 170–78.

Exhibition Catalogues

Architettura nel paese dei Soviet 1917–1933. Milan: Electa, 1982.

Barron, Stephanie, and Tuchman, Maurice, eds. *The Avant-Garde in Russia 1910–1930: New Perspectives*. Cambridge, Mass.: MIT Press, 1980.

Paris–Moscou 1900–1930. Articles by French and Soviet historians. Paris: Centre Georges Pompidou, 1979.

General Studies of the Architecture of the Soviet Avant-Garde

Cohen, Jean-Louis, de Michelis, M., and Tafuri, M., eds. *Les Avant-Gardes et l'Etat: URSS 1917–1978*. Articles by Tafuri, de Michelis, Cohen, Cooke, Khan-Magomedov, Khlebnikov, Gorvich, Borngraber, Kopp, Quilici, and Gutnov. Paris: Ed. l'Equerre, 1979. Parallel texts in French and Italian.

Cooke, Catherine. *What Is Russian Avant-Garde Architecture?* London: Academy Editions; New York: St. Martin's Press, forthcoming 1990.

De Feo, Vittorio. *URSS architettura 1917–1936*. Rome: Editore Reuniti, 1963.

Frampton, Kenneth. "The New Collectivity: Art and Architecture in the Soviet Union 1918–32." Chapter 19 in *Modern Architecture: A Critical History*. London: Thames & Hudson, 1980.

Ikonnikov, Andrei. *Russian Architecture of the Soviet Period*, 75–169. London: Collet's; Moscow: Raduga, 1988.

Khan-Magomedov, S. O. *Pioneers of Soviet Architecture*. London: Thames & Hudson, 1987.

Kopp, Anatole. *Town and Revolution. Soviet Architecture and City Planning 1917–35*. London: Thames & Hudson, 1970. Originally published as *Ville et revolution, Architecture et urbanisme soviétique des années vingt*. Paris: Ed. Anthropos, 1967.

Lissitzky, El. *Russia: An Architecture for World Revolution*. Cambridge, Mass.: MIT Press, 1970. Originally published as *Russland. Die Rekonstruktion der Architektur in der Sowjetunion*. Vienna: Ed von Anton Schroll, 1930.

Quilici, Vieri. *Architettura sovietica contemporanea*. Capelli: Ed. Roca san Casciano, 1965.

Shvidkovsky, O. A., ed. *Building in the USSR, 1917–1932*. Articles on individual architects and related material by Khan-Magomedov, Khazanova, Rakitin, Chiniakov, Gerchuk, Barkhin, Kyrilov, Belousov. New York: Praeger, 1971. First published as special issue of *Architectural Design* (London) (February 1970).

Contemporaneous Writings in Western Languages

"Architektur Russlands." *ABC* (Zurich-Basel), nos. 3–4 (1925): 1–2.

"Architecture moderne et le problème de l'habitation en URSS." *L'Architecture d'aujourd'hui*, no. 8 (1931): 11–16.

Auffray, Pierre. "Architecture Sovietique." *Cahiers d'art* (June 1926): 103–8.

Badovici, Jean. "Le Moment architectural en URSS." *L'Architecture vivante* (Autumn–Winter 1930): 5–50.

Barr, Alfred H., Jr. "Russian Diary" (of a trip in 1927–28). In *Defining Modern Art. Selected Writings of Alfred H. Barr, Jr.*, eds. I. Sandler and A. Newman, 103–37. New York: Harry N. Abrams, 1986.

Barr, Alfred H., Jr. "Notes on Russian architecture." *The Arts* (New York), no. 1 (February 1929): 99–105.

Das neue Frankfurt (Frankfurt), nos. 6, 7 (1931).

Drubkin, A. L. "American architects and engineers in Russia." *Pencil Points* (June 1930): 435–40.

Hegman, Werner. "Lenin-ehrung: Auditorium, Glühbirne oder Luftballoon?" *Wasmuths Monatshefte für Baukunst*, vol. 13 (1929): 129–32.

Ilyine, M. "L'Architecture moderne en URSS." *L'Architecture d'aujourd'hui*, no. 3 (1931): 126.

Ilyine, M. "Le Corbusianisme en URSS." *L'Architecture d'aujourd'hui*, no. 6 (1931): 59–61.

Ilyine, M. "L'Architecture du club ouvrier en URSS," *L'Architecture d'aujourd'hui*, no. 8 (1931): 17–19.

"Les Dernières realisations architecturales en Russie." *Cahiers d'art*, no. 1 (1919): 46–50.

Lubetkin, Berthold. "The builders, 1: Architectural thought since the Revolution." *Architectural Review* (London) (May 1932): 201–7.

Mendelsohn, Erich. *Russland, Europa, Amerika: ein architektonischer Querschnitt*. Berlin: Ed. Buchverlag, 1929; republished 1989.

Seidenberg, Roderick. "Symmetry and ornament discarded as Russia cast off the past." *American Architect* (December 1930): 48–49, 72, 74.

Voyce, Arthur. "Contemporary Soviet Architecture." *American Magazine of Art* (September 1935): 527–35.

Translated Russian Architectural Texts of the Twenties

Chernikhov, Iakov. *The Construction of Architectural and Machine Forms (Konstruktsiia arkhitekturnikh i mashinnykh form)*. Leningrad, 1931. Translated with introduction by Catherine Cooke. In C. Cooke, *Chernikhov: Fantasy and Construction*. New York: St. Martin's Press, 1984.

Ginzburg, Moisei. *Style and Epoch (Stil i Epokha)*. Moscow, 1924. Translated with introduction by Anatole Senkevitch. Cambridge, Mass.: Oppositions/MIT Press, 1982.

Kopp, Anatole, ed. *Architecture et mode de vie: Textes des années 20 en URSS*. Presses Universitaires de Grenoble, 1979.

Miliutin, Nikolai A. *Sotsgorod: The Problem of Building Socialist Cities (Sotsgorod: problema stroitel'stva sotsialisticheskikh gorodov)*. Moscow–Leningrad, 1931. Translated by Arthur Sprague, with introduction by George Collins. Cambridge, Mass.: MIT Press, 1974.

Architectural Changes of the Early Thirties

Bardi, P. M. "La soi-disant architecture russe." *L'Architecture d'aujourd'hui*, no. 8 (1932): 73–74.

Borngraber, Christian. "Constructivistes et academistes dans le Metro de Moscou au milieu des années trente." In Cohen, de Michelis, and Tafuri, eds., *Les Avant-Gardes et l'Etat: URSS 1917–78*, 300–15.

Breines, Simon. "First Congress of Soviet Architects." *Architectural Record* (October 1937): 63–65, 94, 96.

Cunliffe, Antonia. "The competition for the Palace of Soviets in Moscow, 1931–1933." *Architectural Association Quarterly* (London), vol. 11, no. 2 (1979): 36–48.

Khan-Magomedov, S. O. "La recherche d'un 'style national': l'exemple de l'Armenie." In Cohen, de Michelis, and Tafuri, eds., *Les Avant-gardes et l'Etat: URSS 1917–78*, 286–99.

Kopp, Anatole. *L'Architecture de la periode Stalinienne*. Presses Universitaires de Grenoble, 1978.

"Palace of the Soviets, Moscow." *Architectural Review* (London) (May 1932): 196–200.

Samonà, Alberto. *Il Palazzo dei Soviet 1931–1933*. Rome: Officina Edizioni, 1976.

Woznicki, S. T. "USSR—On the problems of architecture." *T-square* (November 1932): 80–83.

Wright, Frank Lloyd. "Architecture and life in the USSR." *Architectural Record* (October 1937): 58–63.

Studies on Individual Architects

Chernikhov

Cooke, Catherine. *Chernikhov: Fantasy and Construction*. New York: St. Martin's Press, 1984.

Cooke, Catherine, and Chernikhov, Andrei. *Russian Constructivism and Iakov Chernikhov*. New York: St. Martin's Press, 1989.

Ginzburg

Khan-Magomedov, S. O. *Moisej Ginzburg*. Preface by V. Quilici. Milan: Franco Angeli Editore, 1975.

Ladovsky

Khan-Magomedov, S. O. "Nikolaj Ladovskij: an ideology of rationalism." *Lotus International* (Venice) (September 1978): 104–26.

Le Corbusier

Cohen, Jean-Louis. *Le Corbusier et la mystique de l'URSS: théories et projets pour Moscou 1928–1936*. Paris: Pierre Mardaga Editeur, 1987.

Leonidov

Cooke, Catherine. "Ivan Leonidov: Vision and historicism." *Architectural Design* (London), no. 9 (1986): 12–21.

Gozak, A., and Leonidov, A., with Cooke, C., ed. *Ivan Leonidov: The Complete Works*. New York: Rizzoli, 1987.

Lissitzky

Lissitzky-Küppers, Sophie. *El Lissitzky: Life, Letters, Texts*. London: Thames & Hudson, 1968.

Melnikov

Starr, S. Frederick. *Melnikov: Solo Architect in a Mass Society*. Princeton, N.J.: Princeton University Press, 1978.

Cooke, Catherine. "Melnikov and the Constructivists: two approaches to construction in avant-garde architecture." In *Russian Avant-Garde Art and Architecture*, ed. C. Cooke, 60–63. New York: St. Martin's Press, 1983.

Vesnin Brothers

Arkkitehtuurin Vallankumous—Revolution in Architecture. Catalogue of an exhibition on the Vesnin brothers. Helsinki: Museum of Finnish Architecture, 1985.

Khan-Magomedov, S. O. *Alexander Vesnin and Constructivist Architecture*. New York: Rizzoli, 1986.

Various Architects

Shvidkovsky, O. A., ed. *Building in the USSR 1917–1932*. Articles by various Soviet authors on El Lissitzky, the Vesnin brothers, Melnikov, Ladovsky, Barkhin, Ginzburg, Barshch, the Golosov brothers, Burov, Leonidov. New York: Praeger, 1971.

Rationalism

Bliznakov, Milka. "The Rationalist movement in Soviet architecture in the 1920s." *20th Century Studies*, no. 7–8 (December 1972): 147–61.

Senkevitch, Anatole. "Aspects of spatial form and perceptual psychology in Soviet architecture of the 1920s." *VIA-6* (Cambridge, Mass.) (1983): 79–115.

Constructivism

Cooke, Catherine. "The development of the Constructivist architects' design method." In *Deconstruction*, eds. A. Papadakis, C. Cooke, and A. Benjamin, 21–37. *Omnibus Volume*. New York: Rizzoli, 1989, (a version of "Form is a function, x," *Architectural Design* [London], no. 5/6 [1983]: 34–49).

Kopp, Anatole. *Constructivist Architecture in the USSR*. New York: St. Martin's Press, 1985.

Quilici, Vieri. *L'architettura del costruttivismo*. Laterza: Ed Bari, 1969.

First Modern Architecture Exhibition, 1927

Kokkinaki, Irina. "The first exhibition of modern architecture in Moscow." In *Russian Avant-Garde Art and Architecture*, ed. C. Cooke, 50–59. New York: St. Martin's Press, 1983.

Architectural Guide

Cooke, Catherine. "Moscow Map Guide 1900–1930." In *Russian Avant-Garde Art and Architecture*, op. cit., and *Architectural Design* (London) no. 5/6 (1983): 81–96.